THE INVISIBLE STAIR
Kabbalistic Meditations on the Hebrew Letters

Samuel Ben-Or Avital

בְּסֵתֶר הַמַּדְרֵגָה
עיונים מעשיים באותיות האלף-בית

שמואל בן אור אביטל

First Private Publication, 1982, by Aleph-Beith Publishers
Revised with a New Addendum in Hebrew, 2003
Three Private Editions from 1982-2009
First Public Printing, April 2016 by **Le Centre du Silence**

Copyright © 1982-2016 Samuel Avital, Le Centre du Silence
Tuesday, April 14, 2016 – Tuesday, 01 of Nisan, 5776

Other books by the author:

The BodySpeak™ Manual (1994, 2015)

Mime Workbook (1975)

Mime and Beyond: The Silent Outcry (1985)

Mimenspiel (1985)

The Conception Mandala:
Creative Techniques for Inviting a Child Into Your Life (1992),
co-authored with Mark Olsen

The Silent Outcry: The Life and Times of Samuel Avital (DVD; 1985, 2015)

Cover design by Samuel Ben-Or Avital

Copyright © 1982-2016 Samuel Avital. All Rights Reserved.
No part of this publication may be translated, reproduced, stored in a retrieval system or transmitted in any form or by any means electronic, optic, mechanical, photocopying, recording or otherwise, without expressed written permission from the publishers.

ISBN: 978-0-9861196-1-3
Le Centre du Silence

KOL-EMETH
c/o Le Centre du Silence
P.O. Box 745
Lafayette, Colorado 80026 U.S.A.

savital@bodyspeak.com
www.bodyspeak.com
www.gokabbalahnow.com

This is the First Printing of the Public Edition.
Offered with love and admiration to members of my family, to my close friends and students, and to all who wish to study these profound wisdom teachings.

Thank you to the friends and family that assisted in bringing to light the Private Edition of this book by their generous contributions spiritual and material.

May all of them be blessed, and may they find divine calm from the Creator and make the heart's Tikkunium, to unite the Shechinah [Shekhinah] and her Maker.

May the triple blessing of the Torah be always in their prosperous and spiritual life.

The Invisible Stairway was published in 1982 and has been studied privately with my students since then. It is with a great sense of festivity that I release this, for the first time, to the public.
— Samuel

TABLE OF CONTENTS

TABLE OF CONTENTS, CONT'D.

ILLUSTRATIONS

Acknowledgments

These meditations and articles were collected from various writings, public and private talks and formed into a manuscript in 1982 for private publication, with the gentle assistance of liana Gali-El (Glassman) and Leslie Colket-Blair.

I named this work, *The Invisible Stairway - Kabbalistic Meditations on the Hebrew Letters.* This manual was created for a few students who needed to learn Hebrew in a certain way so that they would have access to reading some Kabbalistic sources in Hebrew. I added a few instructions for the proper Sephardic way of pronunciation of the Hebrew Letters.

Now some 22 years later, these writings have served privately a few of my students. While revising some of the articles, I found the original Hebrew writings and added them to this newly revised manuscript for those who are fluent in the Hebrew language. Some of the Hebrew articles I translated myself into English. Some are here in their original Hebrew version without any translation.

For the 2003 private edition, my full gratitude and special thanks to Alessandra, (Neshama Bat-Li'Or - נְשָׁמָה בַּת לִיאוֹר) who has studied these writings carefully, editing earlier articles, as well as, the newer ones, both in Hebrew and English.

My profound thanks to my brother in Israel, Raphael Avital (Abitbol) for his kind assistance, and his special letter of introduction about our family for this book.

Also, my thanks goes to Robert Margolis for his kind assistance.

May the Shechinah spread her bright wings upon you and activate her light rays upon your journey into this life. May She assist you in your soul's evolution and restoration, making your Tree of Life prosper with the flame of eternal Wisdom.

Samuel Ben-Or Avital
Monday, Sept 22, 2003
25 Elul 5763 - Rosh Hashanah - 5764
Boulder, Colorado, USA

My Grandfather - R. Eliyahu Ya'akov Abitbol, Z"L

DEDICATIONS

This book is dedicated to my grandfather, R. Eliahu Ya'akov Abitbol, Z"L, may his soul rest in peace. He has been and is a spiritual source of knowledge, wisdom and experience transmitted with love and great attention throughout my childhood in Sefrou, Morocco that had, and still does have, a great impact and influence in my life.*

And to my father, R. Moshe Amram Abitbol, Z"L, may his soul rest in peace, who taught me by example about the important of silence and talking ONLY when necessary, the wisdom of practical and simple ways of living, and, a wealth of other practices that shaped my being to be who I am today.

To my beloved mother, Hannah Robidah Zekri Elbaz, Z"L, who invested all her being and love to make sure I am safe and inspired. Her wisdom stories and healing abilities kept me always protected in her Sphere of the Shechinah - healthy and happy. (Please see, "If All Seas Were Ink" - In memory of my mother, Hannah Robidah Zekri-Elbaz, Z"L.) May her soul rest in peace.

I remember a mysterious behavior of my grandfather, father, and

my mother. They were always smiling and whispering. Their lips always

in a silent motion that I came to understand later in life. It seems to me as if

they were in some constant contact, communicating with an invisible power

of the Creator.

I sensed in their benevolent presence an infinite love that cannot be

uttered but only lived, totally, with great awareness. I am very grateful

for their unique way of gently teaching me the obvious and the ordinary

with such a simplicity which injected great wonder within me always, and, a

sense of the extraordinary.

At certain times in my life, I found myself also smiling and whispering

with gratefulness, the memory of my Sephardic ancestors, who carried

on the Kabbalistic tradition. They recorded with their lives and in their

books, the many treasures of our Sephardic Spiritual heritage. May all be in

peace.

*Please see my family story and biography elsewhere in this book.
Samuel Ben-Or Avital,
Monday, September 22, 2003
25 Elul 5763 - Rosh Hashanah - 5764
Boulder, Colorado, USA

"If All Seas were Ink"

In memory of my mother,
Hannah Robidah Zekri-Elbaz, Z"L.

When I was younger in my mother's house, she used to tell me with great affection at certain times: **"If all the oceans of the world will become ink and all the trees will become pens and the heaven and the earth become scrolls, I cannot describe the way I love you, nothing will be sufficient to express my love to you."**

That unique way of a mother expressing love to her child impressed and impacted my life about the power of genuine love, and since then, I cannot limit the power of love to a word, but, only rather live it, and express it infinitely beyond the ability to describe it.

I never forgot this expression and the good influence of my mother's love = Ahava - אהבה. I found her words so poetic and inspiring, and never knew the source of it, until one beautiful day in my deep study and remembering that unique sense of my mother's love, was reading in the following quote from **Shir Hashirim Rabba** and in another source of the Akdamot Poem I knew from the Shavuot holiday prayer.

Rabbi Eliezer (Ben-Hurkanos) said: "If all seas were ink, all reeds pens, and heaven and earth scrolls, and all men scribes, they will not suffice to write the Torah that I have learned, even though I abstracted from it no more than a man would take a dipping of his painting stick into the sea."
Song of Songs Rabba **1: (3). (1).**

"If All Seas were Ink" Cont'd.

In memory of my mother,
Hannah Robidah Zekri-Elbaz, Z"L.

רַבִּי אֱלִיעֶזֶר (בֶּן הוֹרְקָנוֹס) אוֹמֵר: אִם יִהְיוּ כָּל הַיַּמִּים דְּיוֹ וַאֲגַמִּים קַלְמוֹסִין,
וְשָׁמַיִם וָאָרֶץ מְגִלּוֹת, וְכָל בְּנֵי הָאָדָם לַבְלָרִין, אֵין מַסְפִּיקִין לִכְתֹּב דִּבְרֵי תוֹרָה
שֶׁלָּמַדְתִּי, וְלֹא חָסְרָתֵיה אֶלָּא כְּאָדָם שֶׁמַּטְבִּיל זַכְרוּת בַּיָּם.
שיר השירים רבא א. (ג) (א).

I was transfixed and filled with an immense sense love for all mothers. My
mother was profoundly connected to her spiritual essence. She was a
descendent from a great spiritual leaders lineage, some **22 generations** of
Rabbis, Judges, Poets, Kabbalists and Torah Scholars who contributed greatly
to the community of Sefrou, Morocco where I was born.

And today I say: **"If all the oceans of the world will become ink and all
the trees will become pens and the heaven and the earth become scrolls**, I
cannot utter the profound wonder why most all nations on this earth are again
rising to destroy the beauty of "ISRAEL." No words, no thoughts, nothing, I
repeat, nothing will be sufficient to express my deep sadness mixed with
intense joy at this great world's events and the transition and the great shift
toward a new way of thinking, where every human being will cross the
"magical threshold" to finally realize that there is **ONLY ONE ONENESS** in
all creation and that the **CREATOR IS ONE and NOT TWO**, and death
shall be banished from the life of humans on the new civilization to come."

Samuel Ben-Or Avital, Boulder, Colorado, USA.
Tues, Apr 15, 2003 - 13th Nissan 5763

ABOUT THE AUTHOR

Introduction - Haskama from the Esteemed
Rabbi Zalman Schachter-Shalomi

For classical **sefarim** (books), it was the custom to give a certificate of acceptance, a haskamah. This volume deserves such a writ and not merely as a cover endorsement.

Rabbeynu Shemouel Ben-Or Avital, descendant and disciple of Moroccan Kabbalists, has opened access to the language and content of the sacred Kabbalah and the very studies of the sacred letters for those who have not yet overcome the barrier of Hebrew writing and language. He not only addresses the mind, but also the soul.

Being the master of Le Centre du Silence Mime School, he views the body as the **"Merkaba,"** (chariot) of the spirit, and as a generous soul, readies you for the ride.

May the letters connect you, the reader, to the Great Word.

Yom Shlishi, 17 Nissan 5761.
Tuesday, April 10, 2001.
Boulder, Colorado, USA.

Rabbi Zalman Meshullam Schachter-Shalomi
Emeritus Temple University, Founder of Aleph:
Alliance for Jewish Renewal

Samuel has found an original way
to deeply touch the eternity...

A few words about Samuel and his book,
"The Invisible Stairway"

by Dr. David Passig

There are images in the life of a man that accompany him all his life. For me, that image is Samuel. Samuel is the grandson, and I am the great-great grandson of a great being that was the center of our lives - Rabbi Eliahu Ya'akov Abitbol. Peace be with him, and among all my extended family. Samuel was the connecting link that was between me, my father and my grandmother, Rachel. Peace be with her. (My grandmother Rachel is the sister of Samuel's father, R. Moshe Amram Abitbol. May peace be with them).

I knew Samuel when I was in my early teens. Our paths met the first time when I immigrated to Israel and he came to visit us. The profound connection that was created then cannot be expressed with words. Today, it is a little clearer for me the echoes that connect us.

Both of us drank from the same channels of great ancestors whose learning was the "art of being." Although they traded in commerce to make a living, their heritage and tradition was invested within our souls as great human beings with great faith and connection with the source of life. This man was the father of my grandmother, the great sage, Eliyahu Abitbol. To my chagrin, I did not know him, but, was privileged to know him by knowing Samuel.

A few words about Samuel and his book,
"The Invisible Stairway Cont'd.

by Dr. David Passig

Samuel is the one who followed the ways of our grandfather with his unique style of living and being. Samuel has found an authentic way to express Kabbalistic and cosmic ideas with the medium of the human body. With the soul's means, he has pierced many ways to the great wisdom.

He developed new ways to learn and teach the divine wisdom with an artistic style, and with a rich language that is close to every human heart at the close of the twentieth century and the new twenty-first century. Samuel has found an original way to deeply touch the eternity of our physical and spiritual existence in these times.

As a futurist, in the beginning of the twenty-first century, I find myself trying to touch the same ideas and eternal visions, but from a futuristic research point of view. Samuel taught me that one must find unique ways to touch the eternity within our being. He transmitted to me the message from our ancestors not to be afraid to express our uniqueness, even with the price of being ridiculed by people without expanded vision.

I am certain that our dear grandfather did the same in his time. We are confident to succeed in passing this message on to our offsprings. Samuel's life work contribution will always stand within us as a flame of light and be for us all, a good omen and a shining example as a practical miracle within us.

Dr. David Passig,
Natanyah, Israel,
January, 2002/Tevet - 5762

Dr. David Passig is a futurist by vocation. He is a staff member
of the University of Bar-Ilan in Israel.

He teaches in the Graduate Dept. of Communication Technologies,
and is dedicated to futuristic research of future human societies, and,
in developing new ways to envision various, possible futures.

He heads the laboratory of Virtual Reality in the Bar-Ilan University,
and researches cognitive development with new advanced technologies.

Samuel Remained Faithful to His Roots
by Shalom Kalfon

About Shmuel we can say that he lives the Verse 2:4 from the prophet,
Habakuk:...."the righteous shall live by his faith." - "וצדיק באמונתו יחיה"

His faith in Hebrew is, **(אמונתו)** - EIMUNATO, and his art is, **(אומנותו)** -
UMANUTO. It's a play on words that fits so well his personality. Shmuel
lives his faith as he lives his art, originality and faithfulness. His faith
includes all the gamut of the Jewish Civilization in its colors and richness.
His art includes all facets of art with emphasis on mime.

I have known him since childhood in Sefrou, (Morocco) where we grew up
together, and later in Jerusalem where he started his interest in theatre and
appeared with different groups. Shmuel was always gifted with great talent,
seriousness and originality. I met him again in Paris where he followed
steadfastly his vocation by studying with the great masters of his field, the art of
mime.

I met him again in New York where he was struggling to forge his
personal style in his art. What distinguished him from other artists I know,
is his faithfulness to our heritage, to his roots. While advancing and progressing
in his art, he also followed and deepened his studies in Judaism. He published

essays in kabbalah in a very distinguished and refined literary Hebrew. His essays were published in the Hebrew weekly (הדואר) "Hadoar," edited and published in New York.

I had the privilege to be present in the opening class in Boulder, Colorado, (USA) in one of his international seminars that he conducts yearly. On this occasion, I was surprised to listen to him reciting in Hebrew with such serenity (אלוהי נשמה) "Elohai Neshama" from our daily prayer book. This prayer, we recite every morning, to thank The Creator of The Universe for his gift to us, the gift of our pure soul. In this prayer, we express our nothingness and our humility in the face of our short life in this vast universe. It expresses our faith and optimism in the worth of life itself...

Shmuel recited this prayer with such spiritual intensity that all his students, and I among them, were mesmerized, even though they did not understand Hebrew. They were captivated by the spiritual radiance emanated from each and every word that he articulated slowly with his eyes closed.

Shmuel lives his art and his Jewishness with grace and pride. He has kept his spiritual & cultural heritage, and, has remained faithful to his roots. This is

Samuel Remained Faithful to His Roots
by Shalom Kalfon, Cont'd.

reflected in his many books, which are a spiritual inspiration to all his many readers, disciples and admirers.

In his books, one will find his wisdoms and outlook on life. His theories enclose the richness and the wisdom from both civilizations in which he is so well rooted. His views are expressed with literary talent and with a deep knowledge of the consciousness philosophy. He touches upon the problems of our confused and perplexed generation.

To know Shmuel and to talk with him, one will learn about the richness of his life experiences and his achievements through consistency and suffering without compromising his integrity as a Jew and as an Artist. Throughout his life, he has remained a faithful friend and a genial and uniquely original human being.

Vancouver, B.C. Canada
Monday, Dec 16, 2002
יום שני, יא,טבת,תשסג

Shalom Kalfon is a native of Sefrou, Morocco. He immigrated to Israel at the time of the British illegally. He was a soldier in Israel's war of independence, lived in a Kibbutz, studied philosophy, literature & political science. Is an Author & Educator. Served as a Rabbi & taught Hebrew at the University of Victoria. He was VP of the Zionist Organization of Canada & VP of its charitable fund.

Member of the Board of Governors of the Conservatory of Music. Member of the Executive of the Canadian Zionist Federation & the United Jewish Appeal of Canada. Published books & essays in Hebrew, French and English. He is married to Rebecca and father to Edna, Itay & Vardit.

Samuel Embodies the Wisdom of His Teachings.....
By Mark Olsen

Samuel's work, his life story, and his friendship lives within me as vivid today as it did three decades ago. I met Samuel when I was twenty-two and that year, and indeed, that number, became a pivot point for my journey on this planet.

It was a fine year for me, and that number, like two people praying, resonated in the deepest part of my structure. Samuel embodies the wisdom of his teachings. Samuel understands and honors the ancient technologies that serve the soul, inspiring microchips of wisdom.

From Samuel I learned to stop time, to discover my masks, to relish the invisible, to contemplate truth, to surrender to the void, to laugh and love compassionately. He taught me how to become the author of my life, to climb invisible mountains, ascend or descend invisible stairs, to awaken the artist within me, and, then, devote my life to awakening the same in others.

His invisible world is nourishing and as basic as bread, as symphonic as an Angel, and deeply palpable in the heart. Let his words and the spaces between the words open you like a rose, and the world will remember itself with the sweet, silent, scent of love.

Une chose a la fois. Avec de la paix profonde.

Mark Olsen
Actor, Director, Author
Professor of Movement/Acting
Penn State University School of Theatre.
Pennsylvania USA

Monday, September 8, 2003

ABOUT THE BOOK

The Invisible Stairway
Kabbalistic Meditations on the Hebrew Letters
by
Samuel Avital

This book intends to guide the student in how to work with the Hebrew letters, meditate with them, and learn their symbolic meanings and pronunciations so that the study of the Kabbalah will be practical and beneficial.

It is not an informational book about the Kabbalah, but rather a practical guide, with inspirational meditations on the letters, sacred poetry and stories and affirmations on the names of the letters in Hebrew and English.

Its chief purpose is to prepare the student to become familiar with the letter-code-symbols so that a proper and profound study of the Kabbalah will be beyond the literal. This is intended to stimulate the revelations, the truth of Genesis; to read beyond and between the lines, letters, words.

עֶשְׂרִים וּשְׁתַּיִם אוֹתִיּוֹת יְסוֹד חֲקָקָן חָצְבָן

צָרְפָן שְׁקָלָן וְהֵמִירָן וְצָר בָּהֶם אֶת כָּל הַיְצוּר

וְאֶת כָּל הֶעָתִיד לָצוּר.

"Twenty-two letters He engraved hewed out, weighed, changed, combined, and formed out of them all existing forms, and all forms that may in the future be called into existence."

Sepher Yetsirah , Chpt. 2: 2

וְיֹתֵר מֵהֵמָּה בְּנִי הִזָּהֵר עֲשׂוֹת סְפָרִים הַרְבֵּה אֵין קֵץ וְלַהַג
הַרְבֵּה יְגִעַת בָּשָׂר: סוֹף דָּבָר הַכֹּל נִשְׁמָע אֶת-הָאֱלֹהִים יְרָא
וְאֶת-מִצְוֹתָיו שְׁמוֹר כִּי-זֶה כָּל הָאָדָם: (קהלת . י"ב : י"ב)

"And further, by these, my son, be admonished: Of making many books, there is no end; and much study is a weariness of the flesh. Let us hear the conclusion of the whole matter: Fear God, and keep His commandments: For this is the whole duty of Man."

Ecclesiastes 12:12

THE FIRST WORD

WHO AM I WHO SAYS I AM NOTHING?
"I am not a Human Being, I am a Human Becoming"
By Samuel Avital, Boulder, Colorado, 1982

Who am I? I am nothing. How can nothing say it is nothing? Who is this, I, who says I am nothing? Only constant self-examination can clarify this question. Only self-questioning, particularly in moments of silence and stillness, can lead us back to our source. Only in this process can we cleanse our psychic and physical systems of impurities and restore ourselves.

Who am I? What am I doing here? Almost all spiritual streams deal with these questions, asking us to dare that self-confrontation, that constant search for self-honesty. For me, as an individual and an artist, that search is structured and guided by my study of the Kabbalah, not just on a philosophical level, but as a program and attitude, a way of life and being.

Who am I? For may years, I resisted the realization of the answer to that classical spiritual question. Like everyone else, when I was young, I experienced a strong sense of personal identity: I am something definite, I am so and so, I am a particular someone. Society's conditioning teaches me that you are only your environment, home, school, friends and a compulsive consumer, etc. And this state of affairs is a very limited view of who you and I really are. But even then, the Kabbalah taught me that "nothing" is built in to "I am."

The Hebrew word for "I am" is **ANI** - אני composed of the three letters: aleph א,

noon ‫נ‬ , and ‫י‬ yod. But, change slightly the order of the letters to aleph, yod, noon and you have the word **AYIN** - ‫אַיִן‬ which means "nothing." "I am" becomes "nothing" so easily. Just put the yod in the middle instead of at the end.

So, I grew up being taught that when I said, "I am hurt," I was saying, "nothing is hurt." I am sick, means nothing is sick. I love you means nothing loves you. That was the programing I grew up with, and throughout much of my life I have dwelled on that, and proclaimed it in many situations and experiences, even facing death. And through this, every moment has been intensified with life.

Through this realization, I am focused. I am present. Words cannot explain or express this nothingness. I try to express it by being it, by daring to be myself, by performing it, by teaching it. What seems to be something is actually nothing. I see you. Who do I see? Nothing. Who is this that lives? Nothing. Everything is nothing. But to be nothing, you have to be something. That is the sacred paradox, as is the marriage of all the opposites, male-female, spirit-matter, and visible-invisible.

The Kabbalistic view of the universe is that everything is light. I am a being of light, a spark, encapsulated in this organism, a community of billions of cells working in perfect harmony. This organism is a microcosm, a small world, ‫עולם‬ ‫קטן‬ in itself, a miniature universe that functions in a miraculous way. This organism, this animal system, with all its intricacies and complexities of intelligence and language, communicating between its brain cells and the vastness of the rest of its being.....the very knowledge of all of this is itself the joy of being nothing.

This knowledge is itself the art of living the ecstasy, of knowing that you know that matter is actually spirit, but of a certain frequency, and that the marriage between matter and spirit is the goal, the destination, and the path itself, of the spiritual quest.

Self-examining the self is like looking in a mirror. What it sees in that reflection is the theatricality of itself; that which is and that which is not bemuses it. All life is theatre. My realization is that I play the role of nothing by being something. Nothing sees itself wherever it looks. Kabbalah offers the concept of the image of the broken vessels, שבירת כלים and shattered mirrors. You look in one piece of a broken mirror and you see yourself, you look in another piece and see yourself. Put the pieces of the puzzle back together into one whole mirror, and you still see your self. Every human being is like that. Each piece of mirror, or the whole mirror, reflects the same: I.

When you look at your friend, your mate, your child, who do you see? Always "I," and you see your self reflected in that I. You look in their eyes, and you see yourself reflected in those little round crystals. That is the idea of the broken vessels, the shattered mirrors. So who is looking at whom? Who is it that examines the self, and who is examined? The process itself is very purifying, and it re-strengthens spirituality.

All humanity is like a colony of cells, separate but connected. Separate in order to unite. That is the work. So, when we encounter one another, when we meet and talk, there is work to do. There is recognition: I am Thou, Thou art I. I am not you, you are not I. There is no you, there is no me.

But, we get lost in the cosmic theatricality of all this. These focal points of energy, these units of consciousness, which we call human beings, pretend to be important, separate, and unique. We worship matter and deny that which activates matter, which is spirit. There's nothing religious about this. It's simply a fact.

But, when you know that you are something that is nothing, that you are nothing that is something. You know that every day is a page in the book of life, and that you are the author, the scriptwriter, the interpreter, the central star role, and the actor player of your life. You have the ability to incorporate the ecstatic vision of Omar Kayyam or Rumi and the earthy practicality of Lao Tzu in one breath.

The utterly intoxicated lover of "God," uplifted in ecstasy, becomes grounded and anchored by going from "ecstasy to lunch." The cosmic ping-pong. Otherwise, you can't do your work. That's why the Kabbalah says that the crown is in the foundation (Keter DeMalkhut - כתר דמלכות) and the foundation is in the crown, (Malkhut DeKeter - מלכות דכתר), in the Tree of Life. That's why the heart center, being between, can reconcile what is above and what is below, the knowledge manifested and practiced. The space between thought and action is condensed.

WHO AM I WHO SAYS I AM NOTHING? CONT'D.

If you are at the top of your ecstasy, overjoyed, how can you elasticize that moment and make it last, outside of time and space, unless you live fully every moment, whether joyful or sad? You know it's passing, so every moment becomes a privilege, and becomes everlasting, "eternal." Gam Zeh Ya'Avor (גם זה יעבור) - This too shall pass.

And finally, the wild pendulum of opposites reconciles and comes to a center of silence (Merkaz Hademama - מרכז הדממה) and stillness, neither this nor that. There, you experience emptiness and nothingness. That is quite a learning situation. That's where you "learn how to learn." After the play/performance, you, the actor-player, take your make-up off and return home. Particularly here in the west, we get lost in the left side of our own brains and take life too seriously. We forget to play the various roles that this "I" enjoys playing.

Once we succumb to the "norms" of society, we end up whining in self-pity when we are beset by really difficult problems: "What can I do? I'm only human," the apologist's cries. We enhance the consciousness of our inner poverty, belittling the great being that is within us. That is a crime and a sin. It totally misses the point. It misses the target completely.

Here is then, my friend, a truth without any cover or any hidden agenda. Are you ready to digest it with it total simplicity and illusive obviousness?

Therefore, I declare:

You are a perfect being. You are light itself. There is nothing to struggle for, and nothing to defend. You do not in reality need any approval from others. Your body heals itself naturally. We are ill because our mental distortion of reality interferes with our Natural flow of life - Life as it was intended to be, the state of Homeostasis. <u>A body in homeostasis has no disease.</u>

So, Who is the "I" that resists movement and change? The "I" that can see, in its self-reflection, the nothingness of itself, can accept all of life unconditionally, can reconcile conceptually and practically the so to say "opposites." This "I" can accept totally its own vulnerability. Being vulnerable is the gentle acceptance of life, of one's self. So, what is there to fear? Vulnerability is strength in disguise, the invisible made visible in its opposite.

I am NOT a human being, I am a Human Becoming. Becoming what? That which I am both something and nothing. Why? Because I am aware of "something" in me that I am in touch with, some invisible power that guides me, a source of creation and knowledge where fear and limitation does not exist, something infinite and nameless is guiding every step of my being toward developing and choosing my total expression as a being becoming.

On stage, I am the name that I use, but I say, there is only the play it self, the reality of that illusion, the truth of that lie. And "I," like you, am simply "I," utterly and simply nothing, (Ani Ha'Ayin - אני האין). Go figure that now. Now that I know who this "I" is, the most important question is, How to use it? So, the real quest is this beautiful saying from the wise I learned in my childhood from Pirké Avot, The Sayings of the Ancients 1:14. Hillel used to say:

אם אין אני לי מי לי? וכשאני לעצמי, מה אני? ואם לא עכשו, אימתי?
פרקי אבות פרק, פסוק י"ד

If I am not for myself, who will be for me? And if I am only for myself, what am I? And if not now, when?

We can say. If I am not thinking for myself, who will think for me? Most people let others think for them. And if I am thinking only for myself, then WHAT am I? Or, if I am not acting for my self, who will act for me? And if I act only for myself, then WHAT am I? And if not now, When? If I do not think, speak and act NOW, when? This urgency can motivate us to think, speak and act NOW. Now, this present moment is the right time to think, speak and act. It is a call to eliminate laziness the greatest enemy of self-evolution.

We can heed to this sense of urgency, of the futile illusion of our limited concept of "time" and "space," and appreciate the NOWNESS, the preciousness of this present moment. If not now, When? addresses itself to this noble quest.
I would like to add to this sense of urgency by changing-adding one letter to the word Eimatai, אימתי, the word Ein - א י ן, the negative. And when reading it,

means: If not now, there is no when - ? מתי אֵין, עכשו ואם. A slight change of a letter

can change the interpretation.   Increasing this urgency can even motivate us to dare

to explore, NOW, not later, no procrastination, no escape and no postponement.

Ponder on this practical wisdom and DARE to be yourself in "this" world. BE <u>IN</u>

THE WORLD, BUT <u>NOT OF</u> IT. A gentle suggestion of living a life of a peace and

practical wisdom.

©1982-2003 Samuel Avital
Le Centre du Silence
Boulder, Colorado, USA.

PREFACE

WHY THE NAME

After much meditation regarding the name of this small inspirational book, this verse came dancing around the cells of my being. In deciphering the inner meaning of this verse according to my understanding of its proper translation, I found the essential meaning of "In the Covert of the Cliff." It seemed to simply say, "The Invisible Stairway." Continuing meditation on the verse as a whole, all became clear as to the motives and purpose of the contribution of this book of light and its destiny.

So, the name was chosen -- THE INVISIBLE STAIRWAY (בסתר המדרגה) And since this writing serves as a guide to find the inner ways of the letters, the means to work with them, the hints, and the inspiration thereof to illumination; is like a stairway, a path, a way so obvious that it hides in it, that which is visible. This paradox is a key to this study.

It is like a call, a remembrance, an echo; a call to that which is asleep within us. A call to wake to that inner "voice" and inner "sight." Thus illumined, and through the cyclical regularity of study and, we may discover the spiraling invisible stairway that leads to the source of all, the voice unheard, the ALEPH humming. It is the murmur of the Dove, the symbol of purity and peace, and it leads to Union with the Creator.

Do not be deceived by the simplicity of these writings or the obviousness of the message, for it is from that which is visible, obvious and ordinary that we can decipher that which is, so to say, invisible, hidden and extra-ordinary.

יוֹנָתִי בְּחַגְוֵי הַסֶּלַע
בְּסֵתֶר הַמַּדְרֵגָה הַרְאִינִי
אֶת־מַרְאַיִךְ הַשְׁמִיעִנִי אֶת־קוֹלֵךְ
כִּי־קוֹלֵךְ עָרֵב וּמַרְאֵיךְ נָאוֶה :

שיר השירים . ב: יד .

O my dove, in the clefts of
the rock, in the secret places
of the stairs,
(~The Hidden Stairway~)
Let me see your countenance,
Let me hear your voice,
For sweet is thy voice, and
your countenance is comely.

The Song of Songs 2:14.

45

COMMENTARY

This verse is rich in its teaching content. The mystical name of the Soul is the Dove (YONA - יונה). This dialogue between the Beloved and the Lover depicts the cyclical journey of return toward the "reunion" with the Creator, the Source of Life.

"HE," the hidden one in the cleft of the Rock, the Lover. "SHE," the soul, the Beloved, The Dove, in search of her root which is invisible within her. This verse deals with the situation in which the soul finds herself at this stage of the cyclic/rhythmic/evolution, as she seeks the path to her hidden one.

He is expressing his inner wish to "let me hear your voice." This voice (the Breath) manifested into speech. The word is the vibratory aspect that resonates within her, reminding her of an ancient silent echo. It is through this silent sound that she will find her "way" to "him." The sight is expressed with the "face" that is beautiful. Here sight and sound are united in that realm of oneness.

So, if we reread the verse according to this commentary, we will be reading it thus:

The Lover (male, active) addresses the Beloved (female, passive) to sound the vibratory tone of her spirit, and to show her "comely face," externalizing her beauty, so that after the cyclical vibrations of the path from matter to spirit, unity will be experienced beyond sound and sight.

Or:

I, who emerge from the depths, hidden in the invisible corners of the stairway (stages of evolution) seek thy vibration tuned with me who breathes unto you the life and light; your voice becomes my name and thy name is beautiful.

INTRODUCTION

INTRODUCTION

*"There will never be any explanation of why anything
exists at all. The dogmas of the beginning of a Creation
and a God who creates; will never be anything but futile
attempts to explain away the mystery which is the totality
of time, space and life, and, in a word: being.*

On that assertion, the Kabbalah is founded."

-Carlo Suares 1892-1976

*"I only wish that the leaders of this generation would make it easier to study
Kabbalah...that they would direct the students to the study of the Kabbalah.
Thus no other external wisdom (religion) would be able to raise its head,
and all the philosophers would be cast aside before (the Kabbalah)
as the darkness is cast before the light."*

**-Rabbi Moshe Hayim Luzzato, (RaMHaL) 1707-1746 CE
From: Sefer Yarim Moshe**

Over the years, I have been asked by many students who are interested in Kabbalah, to transmit to them the various universal ideas of this Holy Wisdom and to guide them in how to practice and learn some of the principles, concepts and precepts involved. Kabbalah, a Hebrew word which means to receive, described the ancient tradition of "receiving" the teachings orally.

Kabbalah is the sacred science or a mystical/philosophical system, originally designed to respond to man's eternal quest for the nature of the universe and the CREATOR. As a practical system, it is based on 22 sacred letters which hide in their numbers and forms, invisible cosmic powers and various manifestations of the Universal Laws.

The first step, according to my experience, is to master the knowledge of the letters of the Hebrew alphabet. This involves learning the symbolic meaning of each of the letters, unraveling their code and becoming literate in the Hebrew language. Only through this process can one tap that Sacred Knowledge which is of utmost importance for the concerned being on the path of self-illumination. This guide is directed specifically to those devoted ones, as a means to enter this marvelous palace of light and love.

I am confident that this study will assist and lead the student to a deeper understanding of oneself. With the proper tools, presented in the following pages, one can become the source of one's own revelation as to who we are and why we are here.

Generally, in today's world, the art of passing through a doorway is a common everyday occurrence. One doesn't give to it a very great significance. Passing from one room to another is done as a matter of course, without any particular awareness of the actual physical action involved.

Because of this, there is a reciprocal lack of awareness when shifting consciousness from one state to the next. In order to increase the general awareness of the student on the path of Light, specific attention is drawn to passing through the "door" into the "room," or in other words, crossing the "threshold" of consciousness to find the greater light within.

In the material world, we take for granted going from room to room in a house. Our attention is focused elsewhere. We don't notice the "ordinary" activities without which there is no life. In the spiritual world, one cannot allow this. One must be acutely aware of crossing every threshold, of breathing every breath, of welcoming every sunrise. In the spiritual world, there is a high price to pay for unawareness. The purpose of this book is to bring about such an awareness to the study of the Hebrew letters. If one wants to learn Shakespeare, would one study it in a French translation? The serious student who is determined to glean the inner wisdom of the Kabbalah must first unlock the keys of the Hebrew letters. This book is not offered as information ABOUT Kabbalah.

A suggested reading list provided at the end, provides just a brief sampling of the many publications available which deal with history, terms, places, people, dates, etc. There is also the matter of the scriptures, the writings which compose the Kabbalistic literature.

Any literal translation of Kabbalistic literature will be inspiring, beautiful and poetic, but even these very qualities represent some of the deliberate methods used by the Kabbalists to veil the truths hidden therein.

As is commonly known, it is the literal translation of the Bible which has been the primary cause of the terrible wars, hate for nothing and futile conquering of human over another human throughout the ages.

The sincere student who wishes to KNOW the Kabbalah must first learn to pierce the veil of the literal understanding of its scriptures - to cross the very threshold that keeps the scholars of Kabbalah separated from experiencing the actual inner wisdom which they merely describe with words.

To truly KNOW something, one must become it, embody it, one must go to the Source. If one would puncture the invisible layers of the Kabbalistic onion, one would traverse the corridor of matter back to its source. Matter, as we know it, is a condensed form of spirit, always in the constant state of change, transformation and evolution. It is the visible rendering of the invisible.

Each Hebrew letter in, and of itself, represents a Cosmic power or key which when approached with the proper attitude and correct tools, will reveal itself to the ready and receiving heart. This then, is the first gate. By following sincerely the meditations and practices offered here, the student will find oneself in a state of readiness to receive, according to one's capacity and will, the Sacred Wisdom of this ancient knowledge.

One of the immediate ways to begin to know the powers of the Hebrew letters is through kinesthetic awareness. When we conceive the universe in an integrated way, we learn on all levels of existence.

One of the immediate ways to learn and apply our physical vehicle is through that which we live and be - the bone structure. In Hebrew, the word Etzem, (ם צ ע) stands for bone. This is how we express the self and our existence here in the world of matter and, also, is how we move and communicate.

Bone, (Etzem - ם צ ע), is like the root of the tree which serves as a foundation upon which the trunk is built, and the branches grow into a complete state of being we call The Tree of Life. So, metaphorically speaking, we need the root, the trunk, the branches, the leaves, etc. And water, of course, to nurture the tree to live and prosper, in order to build, create and form the existence of the whole Tree of Life, knowledge, practical wisdom and existence.

The Aleph-Beith Dynamic Movements* (ABDM) is a series of study, working with the Hebrew letters in order to learn their form, meaning, body computation and communication via their movements. Also, by breathing with the particularities of each individual letter, one learns to read and relate to that letter, and, relate to the other letters in this space and time of our ephemeral passage on this plane of existence.

In other words, by moving the letter, you become the letter. These Aleph-Beith Dynamic Movements have been studied live with a few of my students over the years. The essence of the letters is explored and experienced to a certain kinesthetic degree. Therefore, the student crosses the barriers of the physical and enters the state of the SOD (ס ו ד) = Hidden aspects of the letters, exploring their infinite possibilities from that stage of being and becoming.

Think now about this: Self = Etzem = Power = Koah(כ ח). The word for SELF in Hebrew is the root word for BONE, ETZEM which also means POWER. Inside the bone is the marrow which makes us be physically alive. So, when I say "I am," or "myself," I am aware I am referring to my bones, the frame, the structure of my existence now, my immediacy of being.

So, you can understand that <u>the root of our being here is this bone structure we are trying to learn about</u> through the Hebrew letters. Do you see now the connection between "matter"and "spirit?" The importance of you and me being here right now?

When we learn to apply the Aleph-Beith Dynamic Movements in order to embody their powers within our bones, we can begin to conceive, be, think, and live in harmony with lucidity and sanity in this perplexing and insane world of illusion of matter and spirit.

*Dynamic Movement of the Hebrew Letters Workshop Event -
See after "The Last Word"

56

Hence, my developed motto:

שְׁמוֹר נָא לִי אֶת שְׁפִיוּת דַּעְתִּי בְּעוֹלָם מְטוֹרָף זֶה

KEEP ME SANE IN THE MIDST OF MADNESS

This genuine way of exploratory study of the Hebrew Letters, can lead us to embrace and cleave to The Creator. This "Creator" is like a potter relating to the clay, always transforming that "matter" into a new form. Indefinitely, <u>forming the not yet formed</u>, <u>creating the not yet created</u>, <u>making the not yet made</u>, and <u>being that which is not yet born</u>.

Note:
At the end (beginning) of this book, there are some of the Hebrew text of *"BeSeter HaMadrega"* in Hebrew only. This English version is translated partly from the original Hebrew, plus articles that were written in English, and some translated from the Hebrew version, which I added here for those who can swim in the Hebrew language to decipher and enjoy.

Samuel Ben-Or Avital
Monday, September 22, 2003
25 Elul 5763 - Rosh Hashanah - 5764
Boulder, Colorado, USA

LE CENTRE DU SILENCE MANDALA

LE CENTRE DU SILENCE MANDALA
(A Description)

This Mandala was created through an inspiration from the TREE OF LIFE,

integrated with the MA'ASEH BERESHEET (מעשה בראשית) and the idea

of the MERKABA (מרכבה), the Chariot.

Star of David (Beloved of God),

Symbol of total perfection, thou art, balanced between Male and Female,

Aspects of Creator,

Propelled from your center by the 22 Holy letters/elements of Cosmic

forces. Into an orbit of Merkabic energy you sail, wheels activated and

turning, surging onward to the Great Palaces of the THRONE.

AS ABOVE, SO BELOW;

Upper wheel and lower wheel depicting

   The GREAT NAME OF "EHIEH ASHER EHIEH" (אהיה אשר אהיה)

   I AM THAT I AM,

PERPETUAL BEING, ETERNAL, IMMORTAL in all sphere of life/death

   continuum;

Triangles into triangles and infinitum.

The central letters (22) sit on petals of our HOLY ROSE -- symbol of

TRUE ISRAEL (YASHAR with EL - ישר with אל) straight with EL,

name of all names.

Four wheels hold the Circle.

These are the four worlds of the Kabbalistic System--

    Atzilut, Beriya, Yetzira, Assiya.

    (אצילות, בריאה, יצירה, עשיה)

They stand as Guardians of the influx of LIGHT from EIN SOF (- אין

סוף) - The Infinite. Filtering through all levels of life in all matter.

The Kabbalistic adage says,

"ALEPH IS IN ALL LETTERS, AND YOD IS IN ALL OF THEM."

Thus, the idea of wheel into wheel into wheel.   All this activity, dynamic

in its own ALEPH energy, supports and nourishes the Letters in their paths

to manifest visibly into one Neshama (נְשָׁמָה) (Soul). Thus, when one utters

a WORD, formed and created from this activity, one enters the Holy

Ground, upon which the TREE is rooted, and basks in the LIGHT of the

FIRST ORIGINAL SPARK.

Please see this from the multi-dimensional perception of your self, and allow

the seemingly non-existent movement to move you. Thus, with intention

and persistence, one can see the inner movement of this mandala which is

called, the CENTER OF SILENCE (MERKAZ HA-DEMAMA - מרכז

הדממה .)

le centre du silence
m a n d a l a

SAMUËL AVITAL........MARCH 1975

THE PARABLE OF

THE LETTERS OF CREATION

(FROM THE ZOHAR)

פִּתְחִי לִי פִּתְחָא כְּחִידוּדָא דְּמַחַטָא, וַאֲנָא אֶפְתַּח לָךְ תַּרְעִין עִלָּאִין.
פִּתְחִי לִי פֶּתַח כְּחוּדוֹ שֶׁל מַחַט. וַאֲנִי פּוֹתֵחַ לָךְ שְׁעָרִים עֶלְיוֹנִים
זוהר פרשת אמור פירוש הסולם סעיף קכ"ט.

"Open me an eye of the needle, and I will open up to you the supreme gates."
Zohar Emor - Hasoulam 129

"The letters and words are like bodies,

meanings are like the Soul. A letter, a word

not opened, is like a dream not interpreted.

Words without thought is like a foot

without muscle."

Commentary on Exodus 20:1.
Moshe Ben Ezra, c. 1055-1135.
Spanish Jewish Philospher

Throughout the ages, parables and stories have always been an important vehicle used by teachers to impress the memory and awake understanding in their students. A mere explanation may soon be forgotten or brushed aside, but a vivid story will subtly slip into the subconscious mind and be carved deeply into the psyche. These stories, though sometimes comical or nonsensical and often non-linear, always clarify a particular teaching rendering it striking and memorable.

Such a parable is "The Letters of Creation" about the letters of the Hebrew alphabet taken from the Holy Zohar which is considered the "Bible of the Kabbalah." Here, the letters are personified as feminine entities who appear before the "throne of God" prior to the dawn of creation, for the letters had to be in existence in order for Him to speak "The Word."

When the letters address God, referring to him as "Master of the Universe," they speak not of the physical world, as of yet uncreated and unspoken, but of the entire spiritual universe.

The letters appear in reverse order, beginning with TAV, the last letter of the alphabet. "The first shall be last, and the last first." This has a great significance. First, Hebrew is written from right to left. This represents the journey from West to East, toward the heart (on the left side of the body). It also aims toward bringing the intuitive side of the self into proper balance.

Additionally, each individual letter is written from left to right, though the word and sentence is from right to left. Thus, in the process of writing Hebrew, one is balancing both sides of one's self - "the equilibrium balance."

Now, when looking at the actual visible form of the letters as they appear on the page, they seem to be marching toward the left. This I call "the march of the Cosmic powers to the Heart." The letters themselves are dynamic moving symbols. They are static on the page, but they have a life of their own which needs to be realized - when we maintain the attitude of balance in all dimensions.

It is known that the Kabbalistic structure of thinking is multi-directional, multi-dimensional and spiral in its way of relating to the environment and the universe. The letters themselves are essentially circular in motion, the spheres of the Tree of Life are one circle into another ad-infinitum, from within and from without. In answer to linear and one-directional ways of thinking, this Kabbalistic view of the Universe is the path upon which evolution is now advancing. We have witnessed rapid advancement in modern technology, from VCR's to CD's, to the Internet. And now, we are living in the age of microchips & satellites.

In fact, the entire electronic industry itself is actually leading to this multi-dimensional way of life. The computer revolution is gearing toward this NATURAL way of thinking, in which all is related -- coming from everywhere and moving toward any direction one is following at that moment.

If we observe the way ancient Hebrew books are written, we see that the text is in the center of the page, and all around it, on the same page, are references and notes to complete the understanding of the subject. It is as we think it. This is a Kabbalistic computation -- a way of transmitting energy and knowledge. (Refer to the Gemataria, Temoura and Notarikun for three ways of computing and programming the letters to decipher the inner meaning instilled in them at creation).

We have already discovered that the galaxies are circular and spiral, and it has been revealed that DNA is a double helix (spiral). We have also learned that there are 22 chromosome couples (there are 22 Hebrew letters in the alphabet). This is indeed, a very interesting coincidence or synchronization in its own time (the invisible God at work).

DNA itself presents a seemingly miraculous coincidence, as the letters D-N-A are the same letters that describe the "LORD" or the "Master" of the Universe in the Hebrew literature and throughout the Kabbalistic manuscripts. These letters are ALEPH, DALLET and NOUN, as ADON OLAM (Master of the Universe) and ADONAI, ADONEE, etc.

(No wonder why the remnants of the Marranos in Belmont, Portugal remembered only ONE WORD - ADONAY. This word sustained them during their long years of survival; being hidden and invisible until their recent emergence and return back to their Jewish roots with great longing to be with their people.)

These revelations can unite the East and the West, both sides, both hemispheres of the brain, because this nonlinear way of thinking and viewing our universe is wide open and adaptable and always ready to receive.

It is very encouraging to see that all human consciousness, development and evolution is advancing rapidly toward this spiral way of thinking and being, as the Sacred knowledge of the Kabbalah has transmitted to us long ago.

It leads one to be both passive and active at the same time, acting on multi-states of consciousness in a glance of the eye. With this spirit, one can attempt to "read" and "understand" the story of "The Letters of Creation" from the Zohar.

THE LETTERS OF CREATION

"In the Beginning," Rav Hamnouna, the Venerable, commented and said:

We find the first word of our scripture begins in reversed order. **BEITH,** (ב)

in the beginning with **BERESHEET,** (בראשית) and then, the word **BARA,**

(ברא) after it. Then, **ALEPH,** (א), in the beginning with **ELOHIM,**

(אלהים), and the word **ETH,** (את) after it. It is thus, because when the Holy

One, blessed be He, was about to make the world, all the letters were

sealed in an embryonic state, and, for two thousand years, the Holy One

had contemplated them and played and toyed with them. When He

wanted to create the world, all the letters presented themselves before Him

in reverse order.

The letter TAV (ת) advanced forward and pleaded, Master of the Universe,

may it please Thee to place me first in the creation of the world, as I am thy

seal and signature, formed by the word EMET (אמת) and Thou art called by

this very name of EMET (אמת). It is appropriate for the King to begin with

the final letter of EMET (אמת) and to create with me the world.

The Holy One, blessed be He, said to her, thou art worthy and deserving,

but it is not proper that I begin with thee the creation of the world, since thou art destined to serve as a mark on the foreheads of the faithful ones (Ezekiel 9:4) who have kept the law from Aleph to Tav, and through absence of this mark the rest will be dead; and further, thou formest the the conclusion of MAVET (מ ו ת). Hence, thou art not to initiate the creation of the world.

Then, SHEEN (ש) came and pleaded, O Master of the Universe, may it please Thee to begin with me the world. I am the initial letter of Thy name SHADDAI, (Almighty) (ש ד י), and, it is most fitting to create the world through Thy Holy Name. Said He in reply, thou art worthy, thou art good, thou art true, but I may not begin through thee the creation of the world, since thou formest part of the group of letters expressing forgery, SHEKER (ש ק ר), which is not able to exist unless the QOF and RAYSH (ק ר) draw thee into their company.

Hence, it is that a lie, to obtain credence, must always commence with something true. For the SHEEN is a letter of truth, that letter by which the Patriarchs communed with God: but, QOF (ק) and RAYSH (ר) are letters belonging to the evil side, which in order to stand, firmly attach themselves to SHEEN, thus, forming a conspiracy, QESHER (ק ש ר). Having heard this SHEEN departed.

Enters the TSADDE (צ) and says, O, Master of the Universe, may it please Thee to create with me the world, inasmuch as I am the sign of the righteous, TZADIKIM (צ ד י ק י ם) and of Thyself who are called righteous, as it is written, "For the Lord is righteous, he loveth righteousness" (Psalms 9:7), and hence it is right to create the world with me.

The Lord made answer, O TSADDE, thou art TSADDIK and thou signifiest righteousness, but thou must be concealed, thou mayest not be visible so much lest thou givest the world cause for offense. For thou consist of the letter NOUN surmounted by the letter YOD (נ י) representing together the male and female principles.

And, this is the mystery of the creation of the first man, who was created with two faces (male and female combined). In the same way the NOUN and the YOD in the TSADDE are turned back to back (צ), but thou wilt go in another place. She then departed.

The letter PAY (פ) presented herself and pleaded, thus, May it please Thee, O Master of the Universe, to create through me the world, seeing that I signify redemption and deliverance, PURKANA (פ ו ר ק נ א), and PEDUT (פ ד ו ת), which Thou art to vouch safe to the world. It is hence, that through me, the world be created. The Lord answered: Thou art worthy, but, thou representeth transgression, PESHAH (פ ש ע), and for thou art shapen like a serpent who had his head curled up within his body, symbolic of the guilty who bends the head and extends his hand.

The letter AYN (ע), as likewise refused, as standing for iniquity, AVON (ע ו ן), despite her plea that she represented humility, ANAVAH (ע ו נ ה).

Then, SAMMEKH (ס) appeared and said, O Master of the Universe, may it please Thee to create through me the world, inasmuch as I represent upholding, SEMIKAH (ס מ י כ ה) of the fallen, as it is written, "The Lord upholdeth all that fall" (Psalms 145:14). The Lord answered her, This is the reason why thou shouldst remain in thy place, for shouldst thou leave it, what will be the fate of the fallen, seeing that they are upheld by thee? She immediately departed.

The NOUN (נ) entered and pleaded her merits as being the initial letter in "fearful," NORA (נ ו ר א). In "praises" (Ex. 15:11), as well as in "comely," NAVA (נ א ו ה) is praise for the "righteous" (Psalms 33:1). The Lord said, O NOUN, return to thy place, for it is for thy sake (as represented in the falling NOFELIM) (נ ו פ ל י ם) that the SAMMEKH returned to her place. Remain, therefore, under her support. The NOUN immediately returned to her place. The MEM (מ) came up and said, O Master of the Universe, may it please Thee to create by me the world, inasmuch as I commence the word MELEKH (King) (מ ל ך), which is Thy

The Lord replied, it is so assuredly, but I cannot employ thee in the creation

of the world for the reason that the world requires a King. Return, therefore,

to your place, thou along with the LAMMED (ל) and the KHAF (כ), since

the world cannot exist without a MELEKH (King) (מ ל ך).

At that moment, the KHAF (כ) descended from the throne (כ ס א) of Glory,

two hundred thousand worlds began to shake, the throne trembled, and all

the worlds quaked and were about to fall in ruins. Said to her the Holy One,

blessed be His Name, KHAF, what doest thou here? I will not create the

world with thee. Go back to thy place, since thou standest for extermination,

KALAYAH (כ ל י ה). Return then to thy place and remain there.

Immediately, she departed to her proper place.

The letter YOD (י) then presented herself and said, May it please thee, O

Lord, to begin with me the first place in the creation of the world, since I

stand first in thy Sacred Name. The Lord said to her, It is sufficient for thee

that thou art the Channel of My Will; thou must not be removed from my

Name.

The TAYT (ט) came up and said, O Master of the Universe, may it please

Thee to place me at the head in the creation of the world, since through me thou art called, Good, TOV (ט ו ב) and upright. The Lord said to her, I will

not create the world through thee, as the goodness which thou representest

is hidden and concealed within thyself, as it is written, "O how abundant

thy goodness which thou hast laid up for them that fear thee" (Psalms

31:20). Since then it is treasured within thyself, it has no part in the world to

come.

And further, it is because thy goodness is hidden within thee, that the gates

of the Temples and into the ground, as is written "TABE'U (sunk) (ט ב ע ו)

in the ground are her gates" (Lam. 11:9). And furthermore, the letter

HHAYT at thy side, when joined, you make sin (HET) (ח). It is for that

reason that these two letters are not found in the names of any of the tribes.

She then departed immediately.

Then the ZAYN (ז) presented herself and put forth her claim, saying, O

Master of the Universe, may it please Thee to put me at the head of creation,

since I represent the observance of the Sabbath. As it is written, "Remember

the Sabbath," as it is written, "Remember ZAKHOR (ז כ ו ר), the day of the

Sabbath, to keep it holy" (Ex. 20:8). The Lord replied, I will not create the

world through thee, since thou representest war, being in shape like a sharp-

pointed sword or lance (ז י ן). The Zayn immediately departed from His

presence.

The VAV (ו) entered and put forth her claim, saying, O Lord of the World, may it please Thee to use me first in the creation of the world, inasmuch as I am one of the letters of Thy Holy Name. Said the Lord to her, Thou VAV (ו) as well as HAY (ה), suffice it to thee that thou art of the four letters of my Name, part of the Mystery of My Name, engraven and impressed in My Name. I will therefore, not give thee first place in the creation of the world.

Then appeared the letter DALLET (ד) as well as the letter GHIMEL (ג), and they put forth similar claims. The Lord gave them a similar reply saying, it suffices thee to remain side by side together, since "the poor will not cease from the land" (Deut. 15:11), those who will thus need benevolence. For the DALLET signifies poverty, DALLUT (ד ל ו ת), and the GHIMEL signifies beneficence, GEMUL (ג מ ו ל).

Therefore, separate not from each other, let it suffice thee, that one maintains the other. The BAYT (ב) then entered and said, O Lord of the World, may it please Thee to put me first in the creation of the world, since I represent the benedictions, BERAKHOT (ב ר כ ו ת) offered to Thee on high and below. The Holy One, blessed be He, said to her, assuredly, WITH THEE I WILL CREATE THE WORLD, and thou shalt form the beginning in the creation of the world (ב ר א ש י ת   ב ר א).

The letter ALEPH (א) remained in her place without presenting herself.

Said the Holy One, blessed be His Name, ALEPH. ALEPH, wherefore comes thou not before me like the rest of the letters? She answered, because I saw all the other letters leaving thy presence without any success. What, then could I achieve there? And further, since thou hast already bestowed upon the letter BAYT (ב), this great gift, it is not proper of the Supreme King to take away the gift which He has made to His servant and give it to another.

The Lord said to her, O ALEPH, ALEPH, although I will begin the creation of the world with BAYT (ב), thou shalt remain the FIRST of the letters. My unity shall not be expressed except through thee, on thee shall be based all calculations, operations and computations of the world, and Unity shall not be expressed save by the letter ALEPH.

Then, the Blessed Creator of the World, made higher-world letters of a large pattern and lower-world letters of a small pattern. It is therefore, that we have here two words beginning with BEITH, BEITH, BERESHEET BARA (ב ר א ש י ת ב ר א), and then two words beginning with ALEPH, ALEPH, ELOHIM ETH (א ל ה י ם א ת). They represent the higher-world letters and lower-world letters, which the two, operate above and below, together, ALL WERE AS ONE.

AS ABOVE, SO BELOW

AS ABOVE, SO BELOW

The realm of physical manifestation is the perfect double of the realm it reflects. When we perceive the higher realm, we perceive a being of light, ADAM KADMON (אדם קדמון). Every organ is positioned in the physical body for a specific purpose. Every organ is the double of the corresponding organ, the corresponding Sephirot, in Adam Kadmon. If there is a physical nose, it exists as a reflection of the nose of Adam Kadmon, a Divine counter-part. It is no accident that some organs, limbs and glands are double while others are single.

The light pours down from Adam Kadmon into the vessel (See the Cosmic Accordion), the receiver, the reflected physical body, through the SHEFAH (שׁ פ ע) (abundance, emanation) -- a wide funnel. (See Figure 1). Open, raised arms symbolize this funnel; the breathing is the receiving itself, the Kabbalah.

Just as the body here below is the visible reflection of the invisible original above, in essence a piece of shaped space, so are the Hebrew letters space shapers reflecting invisible guiding lines. For example, the DALLET (ד) is made of two lines, one vertical and one horizontal. (See Figure 2.) This is similar to Man, who is vertical by day and horizontal by night. Moving between these two positions in space keeps Man alive. He cannot live without both. There is no physical manifestation without these two states, two lines that meet in a point. But the invisible reflection of DALLET completes the square, enclosing space (Figure 2a.)

Originally the DALLET (see the chart of the four different scripts of the letters) was written with the now invisible third side present, completing the triangularity. (Figure 2b) The third side is still present in the other world. Without DALLET, without resistance, there can be no physical manifestation. It is the principle of flesh, of making, of doing. Nothing can be built or formed without resistance.

As another example, LAMMED (ל) is the connector. ALEPH (א) and LAMMED together from the connecting link. "El" is He, God. "Peniel" (פני-אל), facing God, the Face of God. We find EL everywhere: El Dorado, El Salvador, Elder. El means on, to, or towards. It is the meeting place of subject and object: I go to the house. It is the penis, that which fills the space. It is the place where the above and the below meet. The above cannot inform the below until the below rises to the meeting place. But, the below is incapable of rising until it is prepared. Thus, there is a continual tour et retour --a running to and fro from the meeting place. This is the resistance, the horizontal and the vertical once more.

Each letter shapes space differently, and each letter represents a path in Adam Kadmon between Sephirot. Thus, the letters are guides to different aspects of the invisibility we are reflections of. This is why meditations on the letters ARE the link, the EL. Meditations bring together the below with the above and vice versa.

According to Carlo Suares in his book, "LES SPECTOGRAMMES DE L'ALPHABET HEBRAIQUE," in which he explores the energies of the letters and their anatomy, one can feel and see the realization of INFINITY and the constant movement of life in the letters by their form, and by the cells that compose the letter itself.

One clear example will illustrate this. Every Hebrew letter has a spelling. ALEPH is formed of ALEPH-LAMMED-PAY. If we embark on a journey through this letter we can actually see the great infinity right before our eyes. . . . . . .ad infinitum. (See the following diagram of ALEPH)

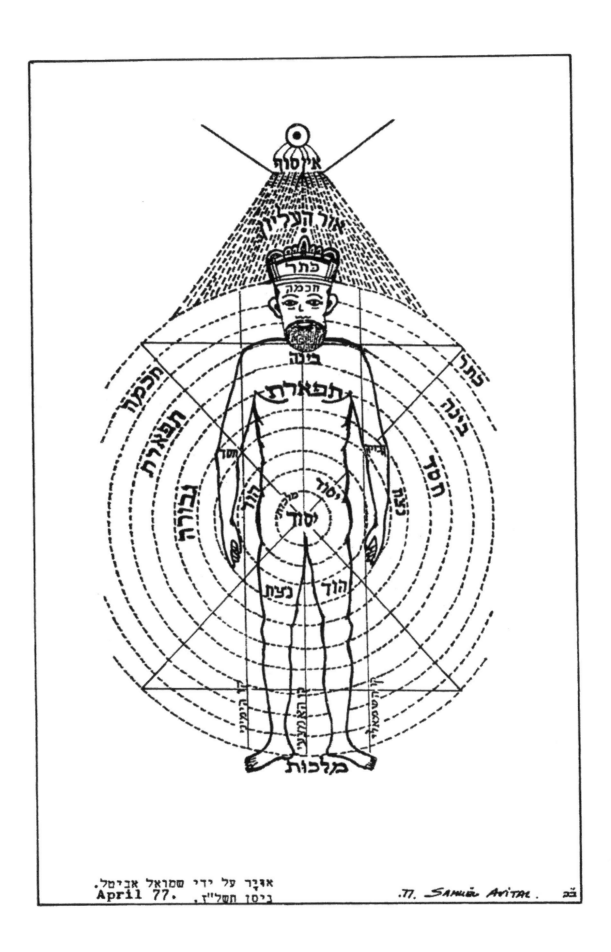

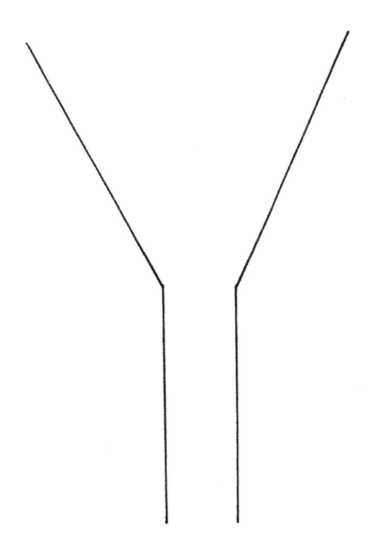

FIGURE 1

FIGURE 2

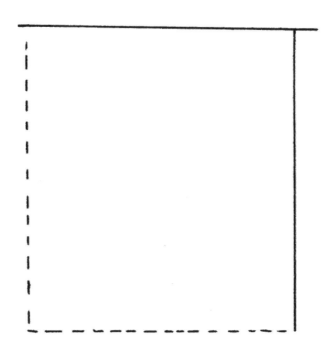

FIGURE 2a

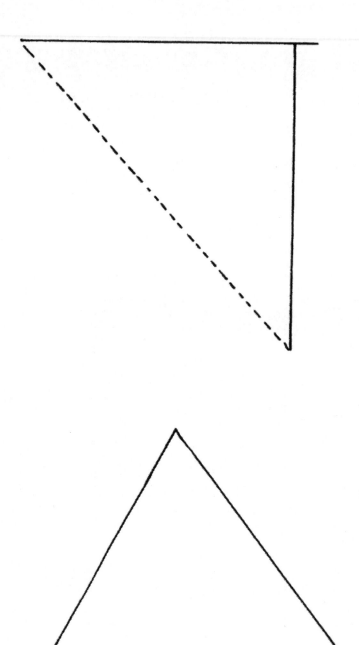

FIGURE 2b

א — ל — פ —··— ה —··—

מ —··— מ —··— מ —··—

ו —··— ו —··— ו — ת —··— ל — ד

מ —··— מ —··— מ — ד

ו —··— ו —··— ו — ת — ל — ד

מ —··— מ —··— מ — ד

ו — ו — ו — ת — ל — ד

מ —··— מ —··— מ — ד

ו —··— ו — ו — ת —··— ל — ד

מ —··— מ —··— מ — ד

ד — ל — ת —·;—

Diagram of ALEPH.

ALEPH:
THE FORMATION OF THE WORD

ALEPH: The Formation of the Word

ALEPH (אלף), we say, has three phases of becoming manifest. It begins
in the throat, meets the tongue in the middle, and ends with the lips.
AH, LE, and FFF. This means that ALEPH is All Life, All Love. We find
this pronunciation of AL in many cultures, as EL, ALLAH, elders, oil.
When the ALEPH is pronounced properly there is much benefit to the
system.

Before being sounded, ALEPH is floating in the spirit of the waters
of the brain. When it wants to manifest, it has to move the organ of speech,
the center of the throat, the thyroid gland, and at the end of manifestation,
it breathes. In other words, the primordial sound AH, which is the first
sound that man utters, the preborn sound that seeks to manifest and
supplicates to be known, meets the middle of the palate, the "lashon"
(לשון) (tongue) where we can say LE, and ends with the lips breathing
out --FFFFF.

"In the beginning was the word, therefore, means in the beginning was
the sound." An unheard sound, before it is uttered, exists in the realm of
the infinite. From that realm of the infinite, it comes to the manifestation of
the vessel, to the organ of speech, and it is uttered.

Therefore, you may have a beautiful idea, but until you put it into action, nothing will happen; it has no life. You can wait for it to happen, but you may wait millions of incarnations. We call this the process of Beresheet -- In the Beginning -- the process of creation. If man is indeed co-creator, he has the ability to create new worlds. This is why talking is important.

It is said that "life and death are in the hands of the tongue."

(מות וחיים ביד הלשון)

If you talk when you don't know what you are saying, you harm your life. We live in a parrot culture; repeating what we hear, instead of, going through the creative process of thinking. When you don't know this, and you lie, you are shortening your longevity. This is why it is natural (of Nature) not to speak when it's not necessary. If you lie, you are abusing the power of speech, the manifestation of the invisible ALEPH. Thus, you come to be visible (or audible) so that the ear can hear.

In Hebrew, the word for mute is Aleph, Lammed, Mem: ELEM (אלם). It means that the ALEPH wants to manifest. It starts with the AH, it meets the tongue, LE, the middle, and when it wants to breathe out the sound, it meets the closed lips (the hermetically closed letter of MEM), MMM. Therefore, the mute man cannot speak. However, if you vibrate the breath after the middle LAMMED, you find the word ELOHIM (אלהים). This is the word that is literally translated as God.

So, if God vibrates in us, and we use His vibration against the law of breathing, we sin (miss the point) against God by acting against the natural process of being and becoming.

The importance of LAMMED (למד) is the fluency of its sound vibrating: le le le le. When people sing they say la la la la. The tongue is the organ which makes the sound go far, undulating infinitely, as the form of the letter Lammed suggests in its dynamic motion.

If the ALEPH alone is pronounced correctly and properly, depending on how many times it is uttered, it automatically causes the opening of that center in the throat, the thyroid. This is very important, because if the thyroid is not opened, the vessels from the top of the head are clogged. This is also important in pronouncing all the guttural letters.

So, ALEPH is sealed from beginning to end. It meets the sound of the breath in FFF. If you take the S from SELF, you have ALEPH left. That S stands for <u>silence</u>. If you learn the deep, profound meaning of Silence, you will have knowledge of Self.

It is said according to the Kabbalah, that the Aleph exists in each letter in different forms, by and through the original form, source, the YOD (יוד), without which no manifested world would be. The following diagram will illustrate the existence of the YOD in all letters and therefore the potential of the Aleph in all of the 22 forms. (Fig. 3)

ח	ז	ו	ח	ד	ג	ב	א
	ם	מ	ל	ך	כ	י	ע
ף	פ		ע	ס		ו	ן
	ת	ש	ר	ק		ץ	צ

FIGURE 3

THE LETTERS
Pronunciation Guide

INTRODUCTORY NOTES

This guide was prepared with the intention of giving the student of the Kabbalah more familiarity with the proper pronounciation of the letters and the words we meet in our studies.

Pronounciation should be initiated orally, but this attempt should be beneficial if the student uses his intuitive ability, and with practice, good results shall be obtained. Being with each letter or word at a time creates an inner sympathy with it, and that opens the doors of revelation to the true reality of the letter or word and its symbols.

For the student of the Kabbalah, all creation is called into BEING by the letters, and also sustained by BEING. He knows that by pronouncing correctly the letters with purpose, intention and knowledge, he invokes its essence. He also knows that every word is the bearer of the covenant between the elements, and it has a specific agreement to combine against chaos.

Today we know the effect of sound on our system. The 8th letter of the Hebrew Aleph-Bayt, HHAYT (ח), for example, must be pronounced from the root of the mouth, and activates, in this way, the thyroid gland. The more it is pronounced properly (we say, it sounds like a sword), the more the thyroid will develop and induce the psychic light within. Thus, the benefit of this study.

Therefore, the Kabbalist takes nothing for granted. He considers all things with deep reverence and humility; writing becomes holy in the sense of "Creating the World" to "write" the "Book of Life."

When this is practiced constantly, the letters become alive, and the actual "writing" and pronouncing becomes a prayer.

We find this emphasis repeated many times in the Kabbalistic material. Rabbi Yismael, who was also a scribe by profession, told Rabbi Meir, "My son, be careful in your work, for your work is of heavenly character. If you subtract or add one letter, you may destroy the whole world." (Erubin 13a). Also quoted in Hebrew text as follows:

בְּנִי הֱוֵה זָהִיר בִּמְלַאכְתָּךְ שֶׁמְלַאכְתָּךְ מְלֶאכֶת שָׁמַיִם הִיא שֶׁמָּא אַתָּה מְחַסֵּר

אוֹת אַחַת אוֹ מְיַיתֵּר אוֹת אַחַת נִמְצָא מַחֲרִיב אֶת הָעוֹלָם כּוּלוֹ
(עירובין י ג.א)

The Kabbalists were known for their purity of mind and heart. Before "working," they would wash their hands, drink water and meditate for harmonious direction so that they would not harm any creature in the world. Thus, they were able to dwell in the mysteries, being here and there at the same time, creating a balance of the soul and body together. All this was sealed in SILENCE.

We hope that this guide will open the doors you need in order to "know" a little more about the holy letters, so that your study will become clearer and clearer in your heart.

MAY YOU EVER DWELL IN THE ETERNAL LIGHT OF COSMIC WISDOM.

Number	Name	Letter		Number	Name	Letter		Number	Name	Letter
1	ALEPH			10	YOD			100	QOF	
2	BAYT or VAYT			20	KAF KHAF			200	RAYSH	
3	GHIMEL			30	LAMMED			300	SHEEN	
4	DALLET			40	MEM			400	TAV	
5	HAY			50	NOUN			500	FINAL KHAF	
6	VAV or WAW			60	SAMMEKH			600	FINAL MEM	
7	ZAYN			70	AYN			700	FINAL NOUN	
8	HHAYT			80	PAY PHAY			800	FINAL PHE	
9	TAYT			90	TSADDE			900	FINAL TSADDE	

THE AUTIOTH אות

HEBREW LETTERS CHART

THE LETTERS AND THE PRONOUNCIATION

This section will present you with the letters, as treated in the SEPHER YEZIRAH, their division and the way to pronounce them.

There are many ways of pronunciation, but in Hebrew, there are two main streams of uttering the letters due to the lives of the Hebrews who wandered for many centuries.

The first stream is the ASHKENASIM, Jewish people who dwelled much in the western world and adopted habits (such as linear thinking) that made them forget the proper pronunciation of their language. They pronounce, for example, the letter TAV (ת) as SAV (ש); the sound of the "T" disappeared. This can cause confusion in the study for one who is inclined to look for the roots of the self. With the loss of the proper way to utter the gutturals, in particular, their pronunciation lacks perfection. Though, it is accepted among the Ashkenasim, it is not the original way of pronunciation.

The second stream is the SEPHARDIM, that section of the Jewish people who were exiled from Babylon to the Eastern countries, and who wandered to Spain and North Africa; some stayed in Egypt, the Arabic countries and the Middle East. They were the ones to keep the original way of the letters (due to the circular, spiral way of thinking which integrates both linear and non-linear modes of thinking). Their gutturals were kept with nearly the exactitude of their ancestors because they did not wander too far from the roots of their civilization. They kept many manuscripts such as the Zohar and the Sepher Yezirah, and passed on to their children the tradition of light which is documented largely among Jewish Kabbalists.

This pronunciation of the Sephardim was recognized by the state of Israel, upon its formation, when the people returned to their land. Radio and television speakers are required to pronounce Hebrew correctly in the Sephardic tradition.

It is according to this tradition that this guide was prepared. The Author, being of Sephardic origin, gives us the authenticity of this work.

Included here is a clear chart of the Hebrew letters, divided into units, tens and hundreds, with the finals and their numbers accordingly.

Chapter 1, Section 1 of Sepher Yezirah tells us that" . . . . .They consist

of a decade out of nothing, and twenty-two fundamental letters. He

divided the twenty-two consonants into three divisions: 1. three mothers.

2. seven doubles. 3. twelve simple consonants."

Chapter 2, Section 1 gives us the names of the three (3) mothers, namely:

ALEPH, MEM, SHEEN as follows:

Chapter 4, Section 1 gives us the names of the seven (7) doubles, namely:

BAYT, GHIMEL, DALLET, KAF, PAY, RAYSH, TAV as follows:

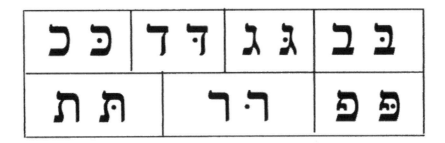

Chapter 5, Section 1 gives us the names of the twelve (12) simples

namely: HAY, VAV, ZAYN, HHAYT, TAYT, YOD, LAMMED, NOUN,

SAMMEKH, AYN, TSADDE, QOF as follows:

י	ט	ח	ז	ו	ה
ק	צ	ע	ס	נ	ל

Chapter 2, Section 3, says: "He established twenty-two letters, Stamina, by the voice, formed by the breath of air, and fixed them on five places in the human mouth, namely: 1). Gutturals, 2). Palatals, 3). Linguals, 4). Dentals, 5). Labials."

1. GUTTURALS		ע	ח	ה	א
2. PALATALS		ק	כ	י	ג
3. LINGUALS	ת	נ	ל	ט	ד
4. DENTALS	צ	ר	ס	ש	ז
5. LABIALS		פ	מ	ו	ב

HEBREW VOWELS

The symbol, □ represents the letter.

Basic Sound	Long (Big)		Short (Small)		Very short vowels	
A	Kamets □	a as psalm	Patah □	a as sam	Shva □	e
E	Tsere □	a as mate	Segol □	e as met	Hataf-Patah □	a
I	Hirik □	as feet	Hirik □	as fit	Hataf-Segol □	e
O	Holam or □	as bone	Kamets-Katan □	as cot	Hataf-Kamets □	o
U	Shurek •□	as fool	Kibbouts □	as full		

Also, a "TREE OF LIFE" chart is offered with the Hebrew names and pronunciations of the Sefirot.

Then, the divisions of the letters are presented according to the SEPHER YEZIRAH.

And after this, each letter is given with its proper pronunciation and a few words to practice written in Hebrew.

In Appendix A, the first few chapters of Genesis have been included for a practical study, with English translation. (The degree of mistranslation of the messages of the Bible is a well-known fact by now, and when you dwell more deeply with the Hebrew letters, you will see how this is true).

FOUR SCRIPTS OF THE HEBREW ALPHABET
THE 22 LETTERS, THE FINALS, AND THE NUMERICAL VALUES

MODRN ACTUL USE	RASHI SCRPT	BIBLE SCRIPT	ANCIENT SINAI	NAME	NUMBER	MODERN ACTUAL USE	RASHI SCRIPT	BIBLE SCRIPT	ANCIENT SINAI	NAME	NUMBER
				AYIN	70					ALEPH	1
				PAY	80					BEITH	2
				TSADDE	90					GHIMEL	3
				QOF	100					DALETH	4
				RAYSH	200					HAY	5
				SHEEN	300					VAV or WAW	6
				TAV	400					ZAYIN	7
										HHAYT	8
										TAYT	9
THE FINALS										YOD	10
				KHAF	500					KAF	20
				MEM	600					LAMED	30
				NOON	700					MEM	40
				PHAY	800					NOON	50
				TSADEE	900					SAMEKH	60

ALEPH is one of the Gutturals: ע . ח . ה . א

and is to be uttered with a light
breathing of the throat. While pronouncing
the AH, there is a light contraction at the root
of the mouth.

Without a vowel, this letter is silent. With a
vowel, it has the sound of the vowel only.
(See vowels page). Thus, ALEPH has three
phases of becoming manifest: It begins
with the throat, meets in the tongue and ends
with the lips. (**A** - throat. **L** - tongue. **F** - lips.)

ALEPH is formed with three letters: **ALEPH,**
LAMMED, PHAY. (פ ל א) It is sealed from
"beginning" to "end." Total in number: 111

Hebrew Form
א
NAME
A L E P H
Number: 1
OX
Literal Meaning

ENGLISH	HEBREW	ENGLISH	HEBREW	ENGLISH	HEBREW
Darkness	אֲפֵלָה	Earth	אֲדָמָה	Father	אָב . אַבָּא.
Finger	אֶצְבַּע	Nothing	אַיִן	Mother	אֵם . אִמָּא
Ark	אָרוֹן	Treasure	אוֹצָר	Love	אַהֲבָה
Happiness	אֹשֶׁר	Guest	אוֹרֵחַ	Elohim	אֱלֹהִים
Emanation	אֲצִילוּת	Man	אִישׁ	Faith	אֱמוּנָה
Lion	אַרְיֵה	Woman	אִשָּׁה	No-end	אֵין-סוֹף
Beloved	אָהוּבָה	Courageous	אַמִּיץ	Mute	אִלֵּם

BAYT is of the Labials: .פ .מ .ו .ב

and of the Seven doubles: .ת .ר .פ .כ .ד .ג .ב

When a dot is placed inside the letter, it doubles the pronounciation. This dot is called in Hebrew, DAGESH - ד ג ש. When there is no dot, it is uttered soft as "V."

Bayt (ב י ת) is formed with three letters: **BAYT, YOD, TAV**

Total in Number: **412**

Hebrew Form
בּ
NAME
B A Y T
Number: 2
House or Dwelling
Literal Meaning

ENGLISH	HEBREW	ENGLISH	HEBREW	ENGLISH	HEBREW
Immortal	בֶּן אַלְמָוֶת	Seclusion	בְּדִידוּת	House	בַּיִת
Basis	בָּסִיס	Crystal	בְּדֹלַח	Son	בֵּן
Problem	בְּעָיָה	Animal	בְּהֵמָה	Under-standing	בִּינָה
Ignorance	בַּעֲרוּת	Analysis	בְּחִינָה	Bright	בָּהִיר
Achievement	בִּצוּעַ	Idleness	בַּטָלָה	Blessing	בְּרָכָה
Valley	בִּקְעָה	Nothingness	בְּלִימָה	Building	בִּנְיָן
Creation	בְּרִיאָה	Exclusiveness	בִּלְעָדִיוּת	Choice	בְּחִירָה

GHIMEL belongs to the palatals: ג, י, כ, ק

and also of the 7 doubles: ב, ג, ד, כ, פ, ר, ת

"G" (hard) with the dot, and **GH** (soft) without the dot, or **DJIMEL**. Since it is the 3rd letter, the perfection of uttering this letter is of importance.

GHIMEL is formed with three letters: **GHIMEL, MEM, LAMMED** - ג מ ל

Total in number: 73

Hebrew Form
ג
NAME
GHIMEL
Number: 3
Camel
Literal Meaning

ENGLISH	HEBREW	ENGLISH	HEBREW	ENGLISH	HEBREW
Border	גְּבוּל	Bridge	גֶּשֶׁר	Great	גָּדוֹל
Fate	גּוֹרָל	Causing	גְּרִימָה	Might	גְּבוּרָה
Decree	גְּזֵרָה	Complete	גָּמוּר	Cycle	גַּלְגַּל
Camel	גָּמָל	Vine	גֶּפֶן	Garden	גַּן
Hidden	גָּנוּז	Genius	גָּאוֹן	Revealed	גָּלוּי
Throat	גָּרוֹן	Redemption	גְּאוּלָה	Sulfur	גָּפְרִית
Grain	גַּרְגִּיר	High, Tall	גָּבוֹהַ	Dummy	גּוֹלֶם

119

DALLET is lingual: ד. ט. ל. נ. ת

Push the tongue to the palate and utter D
with vigor, since it belongs also to the 12 doubles.

The strong one (with the Dot) the weak one is like
the English **"TH."** The Sephardic will pronounce
it as **"TH," THALLET,** lightly on the tongue.

DALLET is formed with three letters: **DALLET,
LAMMED, TAV** (ד ל ת) Total in number: 434

Hebrew Form
ד
NAME
D A L L E T
Number: 4
Door
Literal Meaning

ENGLISH	HEBREW	ENGLISH	HEBREW	ENGLISH	HEBREW
Bee	דְּ ב וֹ רָ ה	Gallop	דָּ הַ ר	Knowledge	דַּ עַ ת
Example	דּ וּ גְ מָ א	Hoopoe	דּ וּ כִ י פַ ת	Word, thing	דָּ בָ ר
Generation	דּ וֹ ר	Tear	דִּ מְ עָ ה	Law	דִּ י ן
Compression	דְּ חִ י סָ ה	Grass	דֶּ שֶׁ א	Honey	דְּ בָ שׁ
Dirty, foul	דָּ ל וּ חַ	Faith, law	דָּ ת	Fish	דָּ ג
Step	דַּ רְ גָּ ה	Worry	דְּ אָ גָ ה	Way	דֶּ רֶ ךְ
Bucket	דְּ ל י	Devotion	דְּ בֵ ק וּ ת	Stillness	דְּ מָ מָ ה

120

HAY, the fifth letter is Guttural: א . ה . ח . ע

HAY is pronounced with a small effort to create VOID. "H" like Home. It holds the middle place between the soft silent **ALEPH**, and **HHAYT**, which is stronger. Both **HAY** and **HHAYT** are the very sound of the breath on a different level of placement.

HAY is formed by it self. No other letters could cause the being of it. It is **LIFE, BREATH**. It needs it self to become it self.

Total in number : 5. HAY is formed with ITSELF: ה

Hebrew Form
ה
NAME
H A Y
Number: 5
Window
Literal Meaning

ENGLISH	HEBREW	ENGLISH	HEBREW	ENGLISH	HEBREW
Narrative	הַגָּדָה	Splendid	הָדוּר	I am that I am	אֶהְיֶה אֲשֶׁר אֶהְיֶה
Sound	הֶגֶה	Honest	הָגוּן	Present	הֹוֶה
Meditation	הָגוּת	Comparison	הַשְׁוָאָה	Being	הַוָיָה
Pronoun-ciation	הִגּוּי	Listening	הָאֲזָנָה	Distinction	הַבְדָלָה
Realization	הַגְשָׁמָה	Vanity	הֶבֶל	Compre-hension	הֲבָנָה
Teaching	הוֹרָאָה	Restrain	הַבְלָגָה	Glory	הוֹד
Esteem	הוֹקָרָה	Expression	הַבָּעָה	Here	הֲלוֹם

121

VAV or WAW is with the Labials: ‫ב. ו. מ. פ.‬
It is as **"V"** or **"W,"** simply pronounced.

Its role is mainly **TO CONNECT**, to serve as a
LINK, to unite letters, words, worlds, etc.

In addition, there are words in which **VAV**
plays an integral part.

VAV is formed by another **VAV**: **VAV-VAV** (‫ו ו‬)

Since it is the connector, it can double it self to
cause the connection. Total in number: 12

Hebrew Form
‫ו‬
NAME
V A V
Number: 6
Nail or Hook
Literal Meaning

ENGLISH	HEBREW	ENGLISH	HEBREW	ENGLISH	HEBREW
Discussion	‫וִכּוּחַ‬	Gullet	‫וֶשֶׁט‬	And he said	‫וַיֹּאמֶר‬
Vein	‫וָרִיד‬	Regulating	‫וֶסֶת‬	And it was	‫וַיְהִי‬
Forever	‫וָעֶד‬	Congress	‫וְעִידָה‬	Veteran	‫וָתִיק‬
Indulgent	‫וַתְרָנוּת‬	Certainty	‫וַדָּאוּת‬	Confession	‫וִדּוּי‬
And the like	‫וְכַדּוֹמֶה‬	Child	‫וָלָד‬	Committee	‫וַעַד‬
Multiparity	‫וַלְדָנוּת‬	Hook, nail	‫וָו‬	Concession	‫וִתּוּר‬
Convocation	‫וָעוּד‬	Curtain	‫וִילוֹן‬	Rose	‫וֶרֶד‬

ZAYN the seventh letter belongs to dentals: ד ש ר ס צ

It is like "Z," simply uttered, making the sound of the bees, BZZZZZ, by pushing the air out through the closed teeth: ZZZZZZZ.

ZAYN is formed with three letters: **ZAYN, YOD,**

NOUN (ז י ן)

Total in number : 67

Hebrew Form
ז
NAME
Z A Y N
Number: 7
Weapon or Sword
Literal Meaning

ENGLISH	HEBREW	ENGLISH	HEBREW	ENGLISH	HEBREW
Pair	ז ו ג	Gold	זָהָב	Splendor	ז ו הַ ר
Coupling	ז ו ו ג	Identity	זֵהוּת	Remember	זָ כ ו ר
Angle	זָ ו י ת	Sweat	זֵ עָ ה	Little	זָ עֵ י ר
Gourmand	ז ו לֵ ל	Old Age	זְקוּנִ י ם	Sunrise	זְ ר י חָ ה
Memory	זִ כָּ ר ו ן	Seed	זֶ רָ ע	Current	זֶ רֶ ם
Singing	זִ מְ רָ ה	Fly	זְ ב ו ב	Erection	זְ קִ י פָ ה
Tail	זָ נָ ב	Insolence	זָ ד ו ן	Caution	זְ ה י ר ו ת

HHAYT is a very important one in pronunciation in the Guttrals: א . ה . ח . ע

It is very sharp and stronger than **HAY** and **ALEPH**. Activate the roof of the mouth, and make the sound of a sword in motion, **"HH,"** a strong exhalation letting the air pass through with vigor.

It is also the sound of suffering, the sigh. The Ashkenasim confuse this letter with **KHAF:** כ In the constant practice of this letter, the Thyroid is stimulated to develop the Psychic light in that area, and in all the systems.

HHAYT is formed with three letters: **HHAYT, YOD,** and **TAV** (ח י ת)
Total in number: 418

Hebrew Form
ח
NAME
H H A Y T
Number: 8
Fence, Net or Window
Literal Meaning

ENGLISH	HEBREW	ENGLISH	HEBREW	ENGLISH	HEBREW
Room	חֶדֶר	Eve	חַוָּה	Charity	חֶסֶד
Sharp	חַד	Lily	חֲבַצֶּלֶת	Space	חָלָל
Joy	חֶדְוָה	Festivity	חֲגִיגָה	Dream	חֲלוֹם
Duty	חוֹבָה	Vertebra	חוּלְיָה	Warm	חָם
Innovation	חַדְשָׁנוּת	Lovely	חָבִיב	Cord, Rope	חֶבֶל
Acid	חוּמְצָה	Friend	חָבֵר	Charm	חֵן
Freedom	חוֹפֶשׁ	Girdle	חֲגוֹר	Experience	חֲוָיָה

TAYT is with the Linguals: ד ט ל נ ת

In this letter, there is a certain roughness
  of the throat. Although it is lingual, the
  sound should be directed towards the top
  of the palate, TTTTAYT.

This is unlike TAV which is softer and lighter.

TAYT is formed with three letters: TAYT, YOD,
  TAV (ט י ת)

Total in number: 419

Hebrew Form
ט
NAME
T A Y T
Number: 9
Coiled Snake or Basket
Literal Meaning

ENGLISH	HEBREW	ENGLISH	HEBREW	ENGLISH	HEBREW
Wandering	טִלְטוּל	Immersion	טְבִילָה	Good	טוֹב
Taste	טַעַם	Drop	טִיפָּה	Pure	טָהוֹר
Patch	טְלָאִי	Lamb	טָלֶה	Navel	טַבּוּר
Humidity	טַחַב	Children	טַף	Ring	טַבַּעַת
Mill	טַחֲנָה	Cook	טַבָּח	Nature	טֶבַע
Fortress	טִירָה	Range	טְוַח	Spleen	טְחוֹל
Pilot	טַיָּס	Peacock	טַוָּס	Dew	טַל

125

YOD is simple to pronounce. Place the accent on the tongue when creating the "Y."

YOD belongs to the Palatals: ק . כ . י . ג

YOD is formed of three letters: **YOD, VAV, DALLET**
(י ו ד)

Total in number: 20

Hebrew Form
י
NAME
Y O D
Number: 10
Hand
Literal Meaning

ENGLISH	HEBREW	ENGLISH	HEBREW	ENGLISH	HEBREW
Wail	יְלָלָה	Day	יוֹם	Hand	יָד
Birth	יְלוּדָה	Crop	יְבוּל	River	יְאוֹר
Basis	יְסוֹד	Sorrow	יָגוֹן	Proper	יָאֶה
Ability	יְכוֹלֶת	To Know	יְדִיעָה	He will be	יִהְיֶה
Israel	יִשְׂרָאֵל	Single	יָחִיד	Creator	יוֹצֵר
Universe	יְקוּם	Aim	יַעַד	Stable	יַצִּיב
Formation	יְצִירָה	Owl	יַנְשׁוּף	Forest	יָעַר

KAF is of the Palatals: ג , י , כ , ק

and also of the 7 doubles: ב ב, ג ג, ד ד, כ כ, פ פ,
ר ר, ת ת

It takes the middle place of the palatals and is
simply pronounced as "K." You will notice
later the difference between this letter and the

QOF: ק

When the dot is inside it, it is **KAF**; without the
dot, it is **HHAF**.

KAF is formed with two letters: **KAF, PAY** (כ פ)

Total in number: 100

Hebrew Form
כ
NAME
K A F
Number: 20
Cup, Palm, Hollow of Hand
Literal Meaning

ENGLISH	HEBREW	ENGLISH	HEBREW	ENGLISH	HEBREW
Nothing	כְּלוּם	Ball	כַּדּוּר	Crown	כֶּתֶר
Yes	כֵּן	Intention	כַּוָּנָה	Cut off	כָּרֵת
Young Lion	כְּפִיר	Vineyard	כֶּרֶם	Honor	כָּבוֹד
Glove	כְּפָפָה	Glass	כּוֹס	Worth it	כְּדָאִי
Writing	כְּתִיבָה	Prison	כֶּלֶא	Mighty	כַּבִּיר
City	כְּרָךְ	Hidden	כָּמוּס	Vessel	כְּלִי
Shark	כָּרִישׁ	Yearning	כָּמֵהַּ	Star	כּוֹכָב

LAMMED is of the Linguals: ד ט ל נ ת

It is simply pronounced as "L."

LAMMED is formed with three letters:
LAMMED, MEM, DALLET - (ל מ ד)

Total in number: 74

Hebrew Form
ל
NAME
LAM M E D
Number: 30
Goad and Learning
Literal Meaning

ENGLISH	HEBREW	ENGLISH	HEBREW	ENGLISH	HEBREW
Turnip	לֶפֶת	White	לָבָן	Heart	לֵב
Office	לִשְׁכָּה	No	לֹא	Dress	לְבוּשׁ
Tongue	לָשׁוֹן	Eli	אֵלִי	Alone	לְבַד
Vitality	לְשַׁד	Loop	לוּלָאָה	Moon	לְבָנָה
Whispering	לְחִישָׁה	Dampness	לַחוּת	Flame	לֶהָבָה
Night	לַיְלָה	Forever	לָעַד	Tablets	לוּחוֹת
Because of	לְמַעַן	Chewing	לְעִיסָה	Lion	לָבִיא

128

MEM is of the Labials: ב ו מ פ
and is easy to utter -- as "M" in English
As the water, it opens with M and ends with M.
Therefore, MEM.

By now, you probably have noticed that unlike
English and some other languages, these letters
have an autography. That is, it is not enough in
Hebrew to say "M," a letter has a name, and a
particular formation that it is made of.

MEM is formed by another MEM, double MEM:

MEM, MEM. (מ מ)
Like water -- no beginning, no end.
Total in number: 80

Hebrew Form		
מ		
NAME		
M E M		
Number: 40		
Water		
Literal Meaning		

ENGLISH	HEBREW	ENGLISH	HEBREW	ENGLISH	HEBREW
Operation	מְ בְ צָ ע	Lamp	מְ נ וֹ רָ ה	Light	מָ א וֹ ר
Anointed	מָ שׁ ו חַ	Conscious	מ ו דָ ע	Water	מַ יִ ם
Scroll	מְ גִ לָּ ה	East	מִ זְ רָ ח	Very	מְ א וֹ ד
Knowledge	מַ דָּ ע	Measure	מַ ד	Manna	מָ ן
Velocity	מְ הִ י ר ו ת	Deluge	מַ בּ ו ל	Pastry	מַ אֲ פֶ ה
Quotation	מ ו בָ אָ ה	Glance	מַ בָּ ט	Tower	מִ גְ דָּ ל
Tangible	מ ו חָ שִׁ י	Cancelled	מְ בֻ טָּ ל	Kingdom	מַ ל כ ו ת

NOUN is of the Linguals: נ ט ל ט ד

It is easy to pronounce. The "OU" here is like the English "OO," like fool.

NOUN is formed with three letters: **NOUN, VAV, NUN** (נ ו ן)

Total in number: 106

Hebrew Form
נ
NAME
NUN
Number: 50
Fish
Literal Meaning

ENGLISH	HEBREW	ENGLISH	HEBREW	ENGLISH	HEBREW
Soul	נֶ פֶ שׁ	Spark	נִ י צ וֹ ץ	Prophet	נָ ב י א
Volume	נֶ פַ ח	Nose-ring	נֶ זֶ ם	Eternity	נֶ צַ ח
Point	נְ ק וּ דָ ה	Pottage	נָ ז י ד	Soul	נְ שָׁ מָ ה
Exhaling	נְ שׁ י פָ ה	Planting	נְ ט י עָ ה	Generous	נָ ד י ב
Roaring	נְ הִ י מָ ה	Boy	נַ עַ ר	Serpent	נָ חָ שׁ
Kiss	נְ שׁ י קָ ה	Exalted	נַ עֲ לָ ה	Agreeable	נָ עִ י ם
Scenery	נ וֹ ף	Unknown	נֶ עֲ לָ ם	Please	נָ א

SAMEKH is of the Dentals: ז שׁ ס ר צ

It is pronounced lightly as "S."
Spelled **SAMEKH**, the last **KH** end in the throat strongly.

SAMEKH is formed with three letters: **SAMEKH, MEM, KHAF** (סמך)

Total in number: 120

Hebrew Form
ס
NAME
SAMEKH
Number: 60
Shepherd's Crook, or Support
Literal Meaning

ENGLISH	HEBREW	ENGLISH	HEBREW	ENGLISH	HEBREW
Rebellious	סוֹרֵר	Knitting	סוֹרֵג	Counting	סְפִירָה
Ruler	סַרְגֵּל	Book	סֵפֶר	Support	סוֹמֵךְ
Order	סֵדֶר	Symbol	סֵמֶל	Satisfaction	סִפּוּק
Stubborn	סַרְבָּן	Apron	סִינָר	Around	סָבִיב
Secret	סֵתֶר	Surveying	סִיקוּר	Vine Blossom	סְמָדָר
Merely	סְתָם	Squirrel	סְנָאִי	A storm	סְעָרָה
Diaphragm	סַרְעֶפֶת	Feast	סְעוּדָה	Drug	סַם

AYN is the last of the Gutturals: ע , ח , ה , א
and there is some difficulty for the Westerner.

The sound of this is similar to the sheep's voice,
activating strongly the root of the mouth, like, **ALEPH**,
but with more accent. A mispronouncing of this letter
can cause confusion in meaning of the words.

For example, **LIGHT**, in Hebrew is **"OR"** with **ALEPH**.
Skin in Hebrew is **"OR"** with **AYN**. Again, the
Ashkenasim confuse between these very important letters.
One must give great importance to the Gutturals in Hebrew
in order to be "straight" with the expression.

AYN is formed with three letters: **AYN, YOD, NOUN.**

(ע י נ) Total in number: 130

	Hebrew Form
	ע
NAME	
	A Y N
Number: 70	
Eye	
Literal Meaning	

ENGLISH	HEBREW	ENGLISH	HEBREW	ENGLISH	HEBREW
Flock	עֵדֶר	Slave	עֶבֶד	Eye	עַיִן
Lentil	עֲדָשָׁה	Past	עָבָר	World	עוֹלָם
More	עוֹד	Circle	עָגוּל	Pillar	עַמּוּד
Season	עוֹנָה	Helper	עוֹזֵר	Cloud	עָנָן
Leaf	עָלֶה	Anchor	עוֹגֶן	El with us	עִמָּנוּאֵל
Joyful	עָלִיז	Eternity	עַד	Amram	עַמְרָם
Heel	עָקֵב	Artery	עוֹרֵק	Work of the Heart	עֲבוֹדָה שֶׁבַּלֵּב

132

PHAY is of the Labials: פ מ ו ב

and the 7 doubles: ת ר ת פ פ כ כ ד ד ג ג ב ב

The law of the dot is applicable here: PHAY with the dot, and PHAY without the dot.

PHAY is formed with two letters: PHAY, HAY. (פ ה)
Total in number: 85

	Hebrew Form
	פ
NAME	
	PHAY
Number: 80	
	Mouth
	Literal Meaning

ENGLISH	HEBREW	ENGLISH	HEBREW	ENGLISH	HEBREW
Cow	פָּרָה	Ransom	פִּדְיוֹן	Miracle	פֶּלֶא
Compromise	פְּשָׁרָה	Deliverance	פְּדוּת	Peniel	פְּנִיאֵל
Linen	פִּשְׁתָּן	Glory	תִּפְאֶרֶת	Fertile	פּוֹרֶה
Wick	פְּתִילָה	Sober	פִּיכֵּחַ	Opening	פְּתִיחָה
Solution	פִּתָּרוֹן	Face	פָּנִים	Clever	פִּקֵּחַ
Note	פֶּתֶק	Passing Over	פְּסִיחָה	Coal	פֶּחָם
Suddenly	פֶּתַע	Paradise	פַּרְדֵּס	Poetry	פִּיּוּט

133

TSADDE is the last of the Dentals: צ ס ר ז
and is pronounced by pushing the tongue
against the teeth to produce the "TS."

TSADDE is formed with three letters: **TSADDE,
DALLET, YOD** (צ ד י)

Total in number: 104

	Hebrew Form
	צ
NAME	
	T S A D D E
	Number: 90
	Fish - Hook
	Literal Meaning

ENGLISH	HEBREW	ENGLISH	HEBREW	ENGLISH	HEBREW
Refining	צֵירוּף	Goldsmith	צוֹרֵף	Deer	צְבִי
Blossom	צִיץ	Trouble	צַעַר	Image	צֶלֶם
Lucidity	צַחוּת	Yellow	צָהוֹב	Just	צַדִּיק
Chill	צִינָה	Code	צוֹפֶן	Rock	צוּר
Jail	צִינוֹק	Need	צוֹרֶךְ	Thirsty	צָמֵא
Expectation	צְפִּיָּה	Dry, Arid	צָחִיחַ	Form	צוּרָה
Contraction	צִמְצוּם	Pivot, axis	צִיר	Bird	צִפּוֹר

QOF is another important one. This should be produced from the back part of the palate near the end of the throat (what we call the root of the mouth).

One needs more effort to utter it -- more than just a "Q" or a "K." Even orally, it is difficult to impart and needs much practice. Generally, when people today utter it, they simply say the "K" or "Q."

This is the last letter of the Palatals: ק כ י ג

Kof is formed with three letters: **QOF, VAV, PHAY** (ק ו פ)
Total in number: 186

Hebrew Form
ק
NAME
QOF
Number: 100
Back of the head
Literal Meaning

ENGLISH	HEBREW	ENGLISH	HEBREW	ENGLISH	HEBREW
Voice	קוֹל	Assembly	קָהָל	Receiving	קַבָּלָה
Monkey	קוֹף	Iris	קַשְׁתִית	Ancient	קַדְמוֹן
Beam	קוֹרָה	Measure	קַב	Bow	קֶשֶׁת
Steam	קִיטוֹר	Community	קְהִלָּה	Steady	קָבַע
Cane	קָנֶה	Holy	קָדוֹשׁ	Line	קַו
Property	קִנְיָן	Blunt	קֵהֶה	Stomach	קֵבָה
Bowl	קְעָרָה	Easy	קַל	Ray of Light	קֶרֶן-אוֹר

135

RAYSH is of the Dentals: ז ש ס ר צ
and should be rolled like RRRRRRRAYSH
with the accent on the RRRR, unlike the
pronunciation of the "R" in English

RAYSH is formed with three letters: RAYSH,
YOD, SHEEN - (ר י ש)

Total in number: 510

Hebrew Form
ר
NAME
R A Y S H
Number: 200
Head, Face
Literal Meaning

ENGLISH	HEBREW	ENGLISH	HEBREW	ENGLISH	HEBREW
Far	רָחוֹק	Sky	רָקִיעַ	Beginning	רֵאשִׁית
Saliva	רִיר	Thunder	רַעַם	Saw	רָאָה
Net	רֶשֶׁת	Mighty	רַב	Wind	רוּחַ
Permission	רְשׁוּת	Calm	רְגִיעָה	High	רָם
Layer	רוֹבֶד	Sensitive	רָגִישׁ	High	רָמָה
Square	רָבוּעַ	Master	רִבּוֹן	Raphael	רְפָאֵל
Ordinary	רָגִיל	Rider	רוֹכֵב	Joy	רִנָּה

SHEEN is also of the Dentals: ז ש ס ר צ and here, too, the dot makes the difference.

When the dot is placed over the right branch of the letter, it is "SH." When over the left, it is simply "S."

SHEEN is formed with three letters: SHEEN, YOD, NOUN (שׁ י נ)

Total in number: 360

Hebrew Form
שׁ
NAME
SHEEN
Number: 300
Tooth, Fang
Literal Meaning

ENGLISH	HEBREW	ENGLISH	HEBREW	ENGLISH	HEBREW
Stillness	שֶׁ קֶ ט	Divine Presence	שְׁ כִ י נָ ה	Peace	שָׁ ל וֹ ם
Laughing	שׂ וֹ חֵ ק	Dawn	שַׁ חַ ר	Almighty	שַׁ דַּ י
Judge	שׁ וֹ פֵ ט	Satiated	שָׂ בֵ עַ	Shabbat	שַׁ בָּ ת
Lion	שַׁ חַ ל	Sublime	שָׂ גִ י ב	Name	שֵׁ ם
Black	שָׁ ח וֹ ר	Spark	שְׁ בִ י ב	Seven	שִׁ בְ עָ ה
Routine	שִׁ גְ רָ תִ י	Year	שָׁ נָ ה	Heaven	שָׁ מַ יִ ם
Field	שָׂ דֶ ה	Equal	שָׁ וֶ ה	Root	שׁ וֹ רֶ שׁ

TAV is the last of the Linguals: ת נ ט ד
and also the last of the 7 doubles: כ ד ד ג ג ב ב
פ פ ר ר ת ת

This is pronounced lighter than **TAYT**. It is the "last" one, the transitional, and thus, the easiness of producing it. The strong one (with the Dot) the weak one is like the English **"TH."** The Sephardic will pronounce it as **"TH,"** THALLET, lightly on the tongue.

TAV is formed with two letters: **TAV, VAV** (ו ת)
Total in number: 406

	Hebrew Form
	ת
NAME	
	T A V
Number: 400	
	The Mark or Cross
Literal Meaning	

ENGLISH	HEBREW	ENGLISH	HEBREW	ENGLISH	HEBREW
Vibration	תְּ נ ו דָ ה	Wisdom	תְּ ב ו נָ ה	Cell	תָּ א
Posture	תְּ נ ו חָ ה	Conscious-ness-	ת ו דָ עָ ה	Simple	תָּ ם
Oven	תַּ נ ו ר	Content	ת ו כֶ ן	World	תֵּ בֵ ל
Movement	תְּ נ ו עָ ה	Pole	ת ו רֶ ן	Naive	תָּ מִ ים
Appetite	תֵּ אָ ב ו ן	Mulberry	ת ו ת	Ark	תֵּ י בָ ה
Symmetry	תְּ א י מ ו ת	The Law	ת ו רָ ה	Mortality	תְּ מ ו תָ ה
Hill, Mound	תֵּ ל	Heredity	ת ו רָ שָׁ ה	Fig	תְּ אֵ נָ ה

BERESHEET -- "IN THE BEGINNING"

Instruction Guidance for

Meditation on the Aleph-Beith

BERESHEET -- "IN THE BEGINNING"
Instruction Guidance for Meditation on the Aleph-Beith

The Kabbalistic tradition holds in its depths many messages for the one who is in search of the Self. It is a well of knowledge that cannot be described until one is swimming in its ocean.

This sacred study contains the great mysteries of the Cosmos and the whole creation. Before entering its magnificent palaces, one must be humble. One must be really hungry to eat from its delicacies. Sweeter than honey is the gift.

The root of this knowledge is in the Hebrew letters. The study of Kabbalah demands a perfect knowledge of what these letters represent in the essence of being. Therefore, if one is to begin on this path, one must return to the source, the Hebrew letters, and recognize the source of being as ONE, by living the oneness and becoming it constantly with every breath.

In this great confusion and world of chaos of mankind today, it is like entering a haven to embark on such a study, shifting from chaos, to order to calm. There is no Knowing of the Kabbalah without the knowing of the Hebrew letters. If you wish to drink water, go to the source -- the source here is the Hebrew letters themselves. If you wish to be informed only, you can read books. Needless to say, there is a big difference between knowledge and information.

There is a vast amount of literature available for this, when one is ready for it. Before even finding a teacher, one must be prepared. So 99.9% of this study is preparation and the rest comes when one's intentions are pure. If one embarks on this ship with the slightest material interest, one loses all the benefits. One must have a map in order to discover the territory.

1. Before every study session with your self, read the invocation (see text) to calm the mind and cleanse your self of everyday affairs so that you can be in tune. Five minutes of total stillness should precede the study itself.

2. First, be relaxed, in a state beyond time and space, and look within the Self, the inner mirror. What are the intentions and the motives? Begin to study one thing at a time. In this case, come to know the form of the letters, the numbers they represent, and master the "reading" of them. Afterwards, the meditations on each letter will begin. Remember, this is only the self-preparatory phase. At first, continue to observe your intentions and to practice silence as a good tool to calm the noisy spheres of the mind.

3. Draw the letter on a big page facing you, or use the letter from this book it self. Become at peace and just look at it for about five minutes. Observe what the letter is communicating to you. This should be done every day

at the same time, spending twenty-two days with each letter. (It is advisable to use the proper order of the letters as they are shown here.)

You will discover that each letter has a power and is a cosmic tool to unveil the essence. Each letter has a dynamic, invisible movement that is difficult to observe in the beginning. With perseverance and intense sincerity, it begins to reveal itself, and that is a clue that the cells are at work and in tune with that letter. Remember, it is only a symbol. Each letter symbolizes a certain aspect of the Creation, the essence of the essence of everything manifested in the whole. A letter is just a vehicle through which this Life Force is presented in essence.

This work should be done with reverence and the utmost sincerity, in the privacy of your home. The letter of each day should occupy you totally. When you observe yourself being idle, recall the letter and its power to chase away the idleness.

It is very personal work indeed. If you are a person who cares, much will come to you. For the superficial, well, all the doors are closed.

4. After the meditation, learn to write and pronounce the letter properly. (A cassette may be available to assist correct pronunciation. Contact the author or publisher for information). In learning to write the forms of the

letters, do not bypass what seems obvious. Sometimes the obvious, that which we take for granted, is where the essence lies. Remember this very well.

5. Along with the twenty-two days for every letter, there should be a steady time to read aloud from the first chapters of Genesis (See Appendix A) for Hebrew-English text as soon as one is able to pronounce the Hebrew letters and vowels.

6. Meanwhile, read some literature about the Kabbalah, choosing some books according to your intuition or from the suggested reading list here. However, remember that this reading is secondary in the beginning. But, being informed is also a form of preparation.

The above are just some preliminary instructions to "shake up the cells" and to begin to breathe with the Order of the Cosmos. The more you prepare yourself this way, the more you will be guided to the "Teacher."

There is no end to any study, and there is no exception here. One enlarges one's horizon by seeking the waters from the source. This preparation is just to bring assistance to those of you who really care for the continuation of life on this aching planet. Every word has the purpose of opening a door to you, the door of return to your source of being. The intention behind this, arising from a convincing knowing, is to put a seed which may grow to be a tree and give forth more life in all.

Following are some meditations on the Hebrew letters which I wrote in Hebrew and which were translated into English, only for the purpose of triggering something in you. So it is second hand, but when you come to know the letters and what they represent, you can swim into the depths of their meaning in Hebrew.

Read the meditations before each letter and memorize them, so that they become a part of you. When you understand the meditations which are here in the original Hebrew, you will make a very important discovery.

Make your self ready for the "Teacher" to come to you. He or she is not going to teach you technicalities. In order to construct a house or plant a garden, you must first have the right tools. Then, with the teacher, you will build the "house" or cultivate the "garden."

May the Zoharic light be thy torch to illuminate thy time spent with each holy letter. Then, they Soul will sing the hymn of Creation with each breath of the Ruah you take. So drink if you are thirsty.

Shalom, from this Place of the Holy Self.

TRANSLATOR'S NOTE FOR MEDITATION PRAYER:

"The following meditation prayer is not a complete
translation, because some Hebrew language nuances
simply are not translatable."

"However, a close adaptation of the Meditation
Prayer was realized. I adapted a certain way
of translation for the English speaking student."

Also, a gentle word of advice! A Tikkun to do before
learning:

"When we enter the Palace of Learning, we shed our
shoes so we can touch and feel the earth. So here is a
healthy suggestion: Leave aside all your opinions,
reasoning and worries. Peel your onion, so, when we
learn, we can make ourselves ready in the Antechamber
and enter the Hall of Learning with a Pure Heart."

"Let the gates of Purity Open Now!"

EMPTY YOUR CUP, SO IT MAY HAVE SPACE

TO BE FILLED......

MEDITATION PRAYER

I will sing the name of the Creator
Who gave me a heart full of Wisdom,
Intelligence and Understanding to be created
with the image of the Creator.
To do and realize your will with a pure heart,
without expecting any rewards

At this blessed moment, all of my being
is full with praise and thanks to you.
I am ready to learn and meditate with joy,
awe and love in the pure and Sacred
Letter of All Creation.

Please my good Creator, Open my heart at my soul
To the beautiful science and
the miraculous being of the Kabbalah.

To the one who formed me, Who is the ultimate good,
Please purify my thoughts so that I can understand and ponder
within the point of the heart today.

I beseech you my Maker, Uplift my spirit in the Bright Light
and illumine my eyes always. To study your Wisdom with Love.
You, the One who emanates Light, my Beloved, strength of my spirit.
Help me to gaze deep within my heart "face to face."
And to manifest and practice from image-theory to action
every day, and teach me to love the "other,"
and receive with good countenance every human being.

Oh my Benevolent Creator, the dear to my Soul
the delight of my heart, object of my delight,
Let me be worthy to receive within this vessel of my resident being
the infinite light of the EIN-SOF of all the four worlds.
And from your Binah Center, emanate upon me
your generous and profound understanding.

Pour on me your ability to understand
without receiving any prize or compensation.
I praise the name of our Creator, and I will sing praises as joy.

Please make me sacred in your wisdom and
open for me all the gates of your infinite capacity to understand.

So Let it be. Amen.

BERESHEET: BAYIT SHEL OR

IN THE BEGINNING: HOUSE OF LIGHT

22 MEDITATIONS ON THE LETTERS

ALEPH   אָ לֶ ף

Blessed El, Lord am I, I have no master

From beginning to end forever the holy wine flows

My mouth would praise one more wondrous than I

I am he.

אָ לֶ ף

אֵל בָּרוּךְ , אֲדוֹן אֲנִי , אֵין בַּאדוֹנִי.

לְרֵאשִׁית וְאַחֲרִית , לְעוֹלָם זוֹרֵם הַיַּיִן הַקָּדוֹשׁ.

פִּי אוֹמֵר הַלֵּל לַמוּפְלָא מִמֶּנִּי , אֲנִי הוּא.

BEITH   בֵּ י ת

My house is whole and blessed by Aleph

Understanding is in my heart

My hand is uplifted to give thanks for the Temple

It is my part to be in Temple-House-Beith in

Joy, Understanding and Peace.

בֵּ י ת

בֵּיתִי בָּרִיא וּמְבוֹרָךְ בָּאָלֶף , וּבִינָה בְּלִבִּי.

יָדִי מוּרֶמֶת אֶל עַל לְהוֹדוֹת עַל מִשְׁכַּן הַבַּיִת.

תְּרוּמָתִי לִהְיוֹת בַּבַּיִת , בְּשַׁלְוָה , בִּינָה וְשָׁלוֹם.

GHIMEL גֶּ מֶ ל

Great and Mighty is He who moves consciousness

in knowing all

Highest above genius of first and last

everything is in Him.

To learn the secret of reward which nurses all,

 all life in Creation.

גֶּ מֶ ל

גָּדוֹל וְגִבּוֹר הוּא הַמְּמוֹנָע בַּכֹּל

מוּרָם מֵעַל, גְּאוֹן רֵאשִׁית וְאַחֲרִית, הַכֹּל בּוֹ

לִלְמוֹד סוֹד הַגְּמוּל, הַזָּן לַכֹּל, לְכָל חַי בַּבְּרִיאָה.

DALET   דָּ לֶ ת

The door to the entrance of Pardes (Paradise)

answering every true caller to the straight way

to the word of wisdom and knowledge,

I will become one and pure with the Creator

for ever and ever.

דָּ לֶ ת

דֶּלֶת כְּנִיסַת הַפַּרְדֵס, הָעוֹנֶה לְכָל קוֹרֵא בֶּאֱמֶת,

לַדֶּרֶךְ הַיְשָׁרָה, לְדַבֵּר חָכְמָה וַדַעַת .

תָּמִים אֶהְיֶה עִם הַבּוֹרֵא לְעוֹלְמֵי עוֹלָמִים.

163

HAY

Glorious and fine the wondrous day renewing

From East soul's rise

The sea living in every path and way right and lit

I was, I will be, for ever and ever and eternally.

ה

הָדוּר   וְנָאֶה הַמּוּפְלָא הַמִּתְחַדֵּשׁ

מֵהַמִּזְרָח שֶׁל עִילּוּי הַנְּשָׁמָה

הַיָּם הַחַי בְּכָל שְׁבִיל וְאוֹרֵחַ הָגוּן וְנָאוֹר,

הָיֹה אֶהְיֶה לְעוֹלְמֵי עוֹלָמִים וּלְנֶצַח נְצָחִים.

VAV　　　　　　　　　　　　וָ ו

Veteran He is

He sees the VaV which unites and Who directs

the fertile Third Letter and makes

Forever bloom.

וָ ו

וָתִיק הוּא.　רוֹאֶה אֶת הַוָּו הַמְאַחֵד

וְהַמּוֹרֶה אֶת הָאוֹת הַשְּׁלִישִׁית הַפּוֹרָה

וְהַמַּפְרָה אֶת כָּל הָעוֹלָמוֹת.

ZAYIN   זַ יִ ן

I will surely remember the seven branches

Foundations of the Creator singing in my heart

the eternity of existence, the movement, the feeling

for all the Good, the Lovely, and the Honest.

זַ יִ ן

זָכוֹר אֶזְכּוֹר שִׁבְעַת הַקָּנִים

יְסוֹדֵי הַיּוֹצֵר מְזַמֵּר בְּלִבִּי אֶת

נֶצַח הַהֲוָיָה, הַתְּנוּעָה וְהַתְּחוּשָׁה לְכָל הַטּוֹב וְהַיָּשָׁר.

HHAYT   חֵית

The vision of Einsofic emptiness free to move through all

In the chamber of Creation, it is like the living sea bearing and freshening,

It will always be whole formed and kept by Aleph and all the letters.

Warm and solid in the heart of the thirty-two paths of knowledge and

wonder.

חֵית

חֲלוֹם הֶחָלָל הָאֵין-סוֹפִי, חָפְשִׁי לָנוּעַ בַּכֹּל

יִהְיֶה תָּא הַבְּרִיאָה כְּיָם תּוֹסֵס וְרַעֲנָן,

תָּמִיד תָּמִים יִהְיֶה נָצוּר וְנָטוּר בָּאָלֶף וּבְכָל הָאוֹתִיּוֹת

יַצִּיב וְחַם הַלֵּ־ב נְתִיבוֹת הַחָכְמָה וְהַפְּלִיאָה.

179

Good He is and Pure, the tunnel of the light of Everlife.

Unique, it is and shining like the one thread to the Almighty.

Its mercy begins in the womb, the place of mercy, the building nest.

Being made, being formed, being created, emanating in the

creations of the merciful and Gracious.

ט י ת

טוֹב הוּא וְטָהוֹר, נְקֶבַת הָאוֹר שֶׁל הַחַי וְהַתָּמִיד

יְחִידָה הִיא וְזוֹהֶרֶת כְּמֵיתָר הַיָּחִיד הָעֶלְיוֹן,

תְּרַחֵם בָּרֶחֶם, מִקְדָּשׁ הָרַחֲמִים וְהַקַּו הַנִּבְנֶה,

הַנַּעֲשֶׂה, הַנּוֹצָר, הַנִּבְרָא וְהַנֶּאֱצָל

בַּבְּרִיאָה שֶׁל הָרַחוּם וְהַחַנּוּן.

Yod primordial knowledge point of the being Principle, the one who

forms, and He knows, and it is found in all the letters and essences.

My blood and intelligence, praised and uplifted living within the

Aleph, the secret of Yetzira, (Formation).

From within it comes the beginning, from it comes the end.

The center of the sphere of the Ein Sof. It will always be: Living in

the ancient being, always renewed.

יוד

יוֹד חָכְמָה קְדוּמָה, נְקוּדַת הָעִיקָר הַמְהֻוֶּה וְהַיּוֹצֵר,

וְהוּא יוֹדֵעַ, וְהוּא נִמְצָא בְּכָל הָאוֹתִיּוֹת וְהָאוֹשִׁיּוֹת,

דָּמִי וְדַעְתִּי וְהוּא יְהוֹרָם וְנִשָּׂא, חַי בָּאָלֶף, סוֹד הַיְצִירָה

מֶרְכַּז הַגַּלְגַּל הָאֵין-סוֹפִי, מִמֶּנּוּ רֹאשׁ מִמֶּנּוּ סוֹף

וְיִהְיֶה תָּמִיד בַּחַי וּבַהֲוָיָה הַקְּדוּמָה וְהַמִּתְחַדֶּשֶׁת

KHAF   כ ך

Palm of the empty hand which works at Craft

Outstretched to receive (for blessing)

Registering every movement, every sound, while turning

The longing heart working in space,

In the enlightened space, sacred place of beingness of Yod.

כ ך

כַּף הַיָּד הַחֲלָלִית הָעוֹשָׂה בַּמְּלָאכָה

פְּרוּשָׂה לְקַבֵּל בְּרָכָה וּמִפְעִילָה

כָּל תְּנוּעָה וְרַחַשׁ בַּלֵּב הַהוֹמֶה וְהַמִּסְתּוֹבֶבֶת

בֶּחָלָל הַנָּאוֹר וְהַקָּדוֹשׁ שֶׁל הַהֲוָיָה הַיּוֹדִית.

Lammed which teaches the knowledge of reward and learning.

Created from the spirit of balance, where the drops of water

are identical; and the wondrous motion of life present within

the Aleph on High.

ל מ ד

לַמֶּד הַמְלַמֵּד אֶת חָכְמַת הַגְּמוּל וְהַשִׁנּוּן

מֵרוּחַ הַבּוֹרֵא וְהַמַּפְעִיל הֲוָיַת הָאִיזּוּן, בָּהּ טִיפוֹת הַמַּיִם

דוֹמוֹת אֶחָד לְאֶחָד, וְהַחַיִּים בָּהּ בִּתְנוּעָה מוּפְלָאָה

בָּאָלֶף הָעֶלְיוֹן.

MEM מ ם

Waters of Life from pure blood of the great Space

From motion in the sea of being;

Without MEM, there is no Mayim - (water)

Within her, life and death, the closed circle of the MEM

and the open; the gone; the hidden.

Concealed in all worlds and hidden within them.

מ ם

מַיִם חַיִּים מִדָּם טָהוֹר שֶׁל הַמֶּרְחָב הֶחָלָלִי הַגָּדוֹל

מִתְּנוּעַת הַיָּם הַקִּיוּמִי, בִּלְעֲדֵי מֵם אֵין מַיִם,

בָּהּ הַחַיִּים וְהַמֵּתִים.

גַּלְגַּל הַמֵּם הַסָּגוּר וְהַפָּתוּחַ,

הֶעָלוּם בָּעוֹלָמוֹת וְהַמּוּסְתָּר בָּהֶם.

NOUN

נ ו ן

A clear soul everywhere and on tune of NOUN's weaving

through everybody, everyone, everywhere

Wakened and wakening for itself from itself.

Everything is in it.

נ ו ן

נִשְׁמָה נְקִיָּה בְּהַאי עָלְמָא וּבִכְלָל הַקִיּוּם

וְהַהַמְשֵׁכִיּוּת שֶׁל הָאֵל, זֶמֶר הַגּוֹנוּם הַשָּׁזוּר בְּכָל גּוּף,

נֵעוֹר וּמִתְעוֹרֵר לְעַצְמוֹ וּמֵעַצְמוֹ, דְכוּלָא בָּהּ.

SAMEKH

ס מ ך

Counted and guarded in the Book

Joined by Vav's rising and perfect, bearing fruit and

multiplying in harvest of the present being. Like the

eternal feminine Rose, Blessed with all, with all, by all.

ס מ ך

סָפוּר וְשָׁמוּר בַּסֵּפֶר, מִתְיַיחֶדֶת עִם וָוין

מְעוּלִים, פּוֹרִים וּמַרְבִּים בָּאָסָם הַהֹוֶה,

כְּשׁוֹשָׁנָּה נְקֵבָה נִצְחִית, וּמְבוֹרֶכֶת בַּכֹּל מִכֹּל כֹּל.

213

Look upon the middle YOD with internal eye

It rises and comes splendid and honeyed

The light of my eyes is my pleasance,

showing the flame in great Darkness,

Showing a world crammed with mystery, glory,

      eternity, and the Highest.

עי ן

עִיוּן בֵּיוֹד הַמְּהוּלָה בַּעַיִן הַפְּנִימִית

יַעֲלֶה וְיָבוֹא עִם זוֹהַר וְנוֹפֶת דְּבַשׁ מִסֶּלַע,

נוֹעַם וְרַעֲנָן לִי אוֹר עֵינַי, הַמּוֹרֶה אֶת הַשַּׁלְהֶבֶת

בַּחוֹשֶׁךְ הַגָּדוֹל, וּמְגַלֶּה לִי עוֹלָם אָפוּף מִסְתּוֹרִין,

הַהוֹד וְהַנֶּצַח הַמְיַיחֲדִים אֶל עֶלְיוֹן.

PHAY

My mouth is open to speak my book

of being kept in breath's dwelling.

My mouth praises joy, glory, and beauty

of the middle pillar, the only, and God giving life.

פ ה

פִּי פָּתוּחַ לְדַבֵּר אֶת פָּרָשַׁת קִיּוּמִי

הַשָּׁמוּר בְּמִשְׁכַּן הַנְּשִׁימָה, וּפִי יַגִּיד דְּבָרוֹ

וְשִׂשׂוֹן לִבִּי, הוֹדוֹ וַהֲדָרוֹ שֶׁל הָעַמּוּד הָאֶמְצָעִי

הַמְיוּחָד בּוֹ וְהַמְחַוְיָאֶל.

TSADDE

צ ד י

Justice weighed in my heart from my mother's womb,

teaching me:

Wide open doors for YAH! who spreads over me

the blanket of peace.

Rock of my world, within me shines

His light and splendor. Just, pure, and complete.

צ ד י

צֶדֶק מְאוּזָן בְּלִבִּי מֵרֶחֶם אִמִּי, מְלַמֵּד אוֹתִי, וּפוֹתֵחַ

דְּלָתוֹת פְּתוּחוֹת לִרְוָחָה לְקַבֵּל יָה

וְהוּא יִפְרוֹשׁ עָלַי סוּכַּת שְׁלוֹמוֹ, צוּר עוֹלָמִי,

בִּי זוֹהֵר אוֹרוֹ הַצַּדִּיק וְהַתָּם, כָּלִיל.

ק ו ף

Was before All, Ancient Before Being,

Sacred to rising, and to the stature. Fast for

the spirit to awaken. I call the day sacred here,

and only here. It resembles head and beard.

My Qof, body and soul are one.

ק ו ף

קֶדֶם הוּא לַכֹּל, קַדְמוֹן הוּא לַהֲוָיָה, קָדוֹשׁ לַקִּימָה וְלַקּוֹמָה.

וּמָהִיר לְהִתְעוֹרְרוּת הָרוּחַ, אֶקְרָא יוֹם קָדוֹשׁ.

פֹּה וְרַק פֹּה דּוֹמֶה לְאַחֲרִית רֹאשׁ וְזָקָן,

קוּפִי גוּפִי, וְנִשְׁמָתִי חַד הוּא.

RAYSH

Head in Being and Nothing, high and merciful,

Contains the yods of Beresheet in it

and wine head full of light always building by the spirit of all souls

an unceasing motion of being.

ר י ש

רֹאשׁ בְּיֵשׁ וּבַאַיִן, רָם, רַחוּם וּמֵכִיל

יוֹדִין שֶׁל בְּרֵאשִׁית וְיַיִן, רֹאשׁ מָלֵא אוֹר

שִׁיכּוּן תָּמִיד בָּרוּחַ שֶׁל כָּל הַנְּשָׁמוֹת בִּתְנוּעָה

תְּמִידִית שֶׁל הַהֲוָיָה.

237

SHEEN

ש י ן

Teaching, hearing gift of complete joy

The Spirit of God in it - inhaling and exhaling

Breathing its voice heard at dawns of secret,

Shaddai, Highest El

Watching it as His precious eye.

ש י ן

שִׁנּוּן הַשְּׁמִיעָה, שַׁי הַשָּׂשׂוֹן הַשָּׁלֵם.

יֵשׁ בָּה רוּחַ אֱלֹהִים, הַנּוֹשֶׁמֶת וּמַנְשִׁימָה,

נִשְׁמַע קוֹלָהּ בְּשַׁחֲקֵי רָז, שַׁדַּי אֵל עֶלְיוֹן,

שׁוֹמֵר הוּא כְּבָבַת עֵינוֹ.

241

Whole and Ever complete, letter of Truth and death,

the mother of all life,

Of peace, wholeness, perfection, completion.

End and beginning, beginning and end.

Open room to all and my words you hear and sing,

the nothing in it and the end - FOS NYA (FOSNYA)

wondrous Aleph, the High in I.

ת ו

תָּם וְתָמִים נִשְׁלָם, אוֹת -שֶׁל אֱמֶת וּמָוֶת,

שֶׁל אֵם כָּל חַי, שֶׁל שָׁלוֹם, שְׁלֵמוּת וְסִיּוּם

קֵץ וְסוֹף-שֶׁהוּא-רֵאשִׁית, תָּא פָּתוּחַ לַכֹּל וּבַכֹּל.

וְאֶת דִּבְרֵי עֶלְיוֹן תִּשְׁמַע וְתַאֲזִין,

בָּה הָאַיִן וְהַסּוֹף, הָאוֹת וְהַסִּימָן לְכָל חַי.

פוֹסְנְיָא שֶׁל אָלֶף הַמּוּפְלָא וְהָרָם בַּאֲנִי.

THE 22 LETTERS: SYMBOLIC MEANING

ALEPH   א ל ף

Symbolizes the original essence, visible and invisible, of ALL.

Timeless in time, spaceless in space. Here, there, beyond, life,

death, beyond. The nameless of the name of all conceivable

and inconceivable, light of all symbols, beyond consciousness.

Consciously manifested to the eyes that know to see the

unlimited infinite.

BEITH   ב י ת

That which contains all the essence,

Receptacle of the invisible-visible.

Without it, there is no life-death continuum.

The cup, the heart, the curve, the circle, etc.

GHIMEL

ג י מ ל

The movement of the inner circle-container, the place or

laboratory of change and transmutation. Transformer of

all that is, digestion of the life in action.

DALLET

ד ל ת

The life response of transformation. Firm square. Resistance without which there is no existence. Crystallization of ideas and activities. Nutritional functioning, in harmony and resolving conflicts.

HAY   ה

Universal life in the process of transforming.

In the container with the "Holy Paradox" of

conflict-harmony, it exists without rational proof,

in spite of all else. Does not need explanation. It

is in all levels of vibrational life. Nothing is

without it, and all is without it.

VAV ו ו

Connecting link to all life, impregnating agent.

Fertility tool, impregnating ideas into action.

Reproductive organs in all forms of life. Its

motion is obvious, in the small world and the

big world.

ZAYN   ז י ן

The vital impregnation bears fruit, infinite

possibilities of untapped energy. Immense potential

for restructuring energy in everything that is in the

process of birth and rebirth.

HHAYT ח י ת

Storage sphere of all unborn forms of energy. A

probable balance at work. Collective unconscious,

possible projections of thoughts and energetic action

to become. All is in the potential.

TAYT   ט י ת

Archetype of the female energy, corresponding to VAV

and ZAYN. The womb in which the organic cell works

its path towards manifestation. A building nest of all

life completed in the 9th path of wisdom in action.

YOD   י ו ד

The original dot even before the ALEPH from which

ALL is being born and dies. Infinite principle of all

ways to measure the immeasurable. That which can

be nurtured by hand, visible and invisible. The center

of the sphere, unlimited, first and last of all.

KAF   כ ף

Cup, container second to BAYT with same functions,

but in the actual way of material life. Contains visibly

all the possibilities, big or small. Water source, life

support, in the actual reality.

LAMMED ל מ ד

The actual, organic manifestation of GHIMEL,

also connecting link in the third sphere, spiritual

"breath" of life.

MEM   מ ם

Second to DALLET. The waters of life flowing

through any container that can obtain its contents

in the invisible and in the visible. The waters-blood

in the resistant - DALLET, making a harmonious

place of being and becoming.

NOUN   נ ו ן

The manifested life forms of the symbol of HAY.

From an invisible dot in fertilization, from the seed,

comes the plant, or consciousness. A condensation

of HAY into this plane of immediate being.

SAMEKH   ס מ ך

The female aspect of VAV, place for fertilization. The

eternal "LADY ROSE CIRCLE," that which holds the seed

and transforms it into a female actuality to respond to the

VAV symbol. A support to the call for regeneration.

AYN   עֶ י ן

The place of vision, after fertilization. The eye

that sees all, to explore with its infinite capacity

the great world and the small world. With the

invisible YOD's guidance it embraces all life.

PHAY   פ ה

The organ of ORAL life work. Mouth, tool of

expressing with Breath-Voice, to form symbol

into word communication. Life and death in

its choice. Ideas to be born have to be formulated

with the ability of speech. One of the nine hole -

spaces of the human-body-unit of consciousness.

TSADDE   צ ד י

The transfigured female form from the work of TAYT. The

Bloomed ROSE - Female greeting the SUN-LIGHT. That which

contains in it the seed and the fruit, in potential. Continuity of

the Human experiment in the planet's evolution.

QOF   ק ו ף

The fulfillment of the YOD and the ALEPH

on a grand scale of vibrational life everywhere.

A completion of the great work of the invisible

ALEPH and the actual-visible YOD. The

complete Man-Woman Being.

RAYSH   ר י שׁ

The higher cosmic container, the place of

achievement that contains the uncontained.

TOTAL PARADOX contained in a place called

NOTHING. Beyond human conception, the third

sphere of KHAF and BAYT.

SHEEN   שׁ י ן

The three great flames that consume the works

of LAMMED and GHIMEL. On all levels, the

fire without which there is no transformation.

The three pillars of BECOMING organically

alive, accepting the principle of the TRIANGLE.

TAV   ת ו

The total completion of the works of MEM and

DALLET. Cannot describe itself, because it is

the perfection in action that puzzles man.

Therefore, an ideal of perfection at work. Can

only be experienced in "Etat de Grace." In it, all

goes back to its source.

22 AFFIRMATIONS: NAMES AND LETTERS

Inspired through meditation, these affirmations on each letter are to assist you in further comprehending the inner meanings of the letters.

Each letter has a "guardian angel," the spelling of its name beginning with the letter itself and ending with the holy syllable "EL." For example, the "guardian angel" of ALEPH is AVIEL: It begins with the letter Aleph and ends with EL.

Through meditation, you shall actually find the inner revelation of the meaning and function of the "guardian angel." This takes place on the celestial level passing through the formation of the word.

Learn these affirmations by heart and repeat them to yourself. When you work and meditate with each letter, let this affirmation be your guide to the inner realms. In this way, you may provoke from that inner level your own revelations.

May the power and love of ALEPH be with you.

TABLE OF NAMES

LAHAVIEL	ל	להביאל	AVIEL	א	אביאל
MEROMIEL	מ	מרומיאל	BENIEL	ב	בניאל
NETANUEL	נ	נתניאל	GAMLIEL	ג	גמליאל
SAHARIEL	ס	סהריאל	DEGLIEL	ד	דגליאל
OLAMIEL	ע	עולמיאל	HADRIEL	ה	הדריאל
PARDESIEL	פ	פרדסיאל	VARDIEL	ו	ורדיאל
TZIDKATIEL	צ	צדקתיאל	ZEMRIEL	ז	זמריאל
KOLIEL	ק	קוליאל	HANIEL	ח	חניאל
RAMUEL	ר	רמואל	TUVIEL	ט	טוביאל
SHELOMIEL	ש	שלומיאל	YEMUEL	י	ימואל
TAMIEL	ת	תמיאל	KETERIEL	כ	כתריאל

AVIEL   אביאל

My being is contained in the essence of the Creator.

The El that permeates all, the Father of all, MALE-

FEMALE energy is functioning harmoniously in ME.

BENIEL   בניאל

My being is the son of Father, infinitely small,

infinitely great. In HIM, I am One. HE-SHE are

one in this contained house I inhabit.

GAMLIEL   גמליאל

It is given to me as I give to others. Harmony

is the place of becoming creative. This thought

strengthens me at all times with Peace and

Prosperity.

DEGLIEL   דגליאל

His spirit is my banner by which I remember

from where I come and to where I go. Knowing

that all places are the first and the last, my

banner of Oneness is with me all ways.

HADRIEL   הדריאל

The splendor of EL is with me, to regenerate

me wherever I need strength, and to be contained

in me with the everlasting Peace and LIGHT.

VARDIEL ורדיאל

The Rose of My Heart is planted in the El

of me while I am dwelling with the scent of

the ROSE. With the SUN LIGHT, I am being

and becoming ONE in all the Universe.

ZEMRIEL   זמריאל

In this ME, the primal note of sound reverberates,

in all my being. Knowing His tune, I immerse

myself in all the cells of this body that contain the

spirit of singing His greatness to all.

HANIEL   חניאל

The merciful One of El always watching me with

the eye of charm and Grace, the influx of wisdom

permeating every cell of my being. MERCY and

Courage are the message of this day of LIGHT.

TUVIEL טוביאל

The goodness of El is my birthright while passing through

the density of this vessel called body. Visibly and invisibly

I declare the goodness to guide my thoughts and action this

day of good.

YEMOUEL   יְמוּאֵל

The Ocean of being in EL in which I am guided to

swim. Every drop makes the sea, all the sea is

from all drops of every cell. Flowing waters of life

and energetic action are in me.

KETERIEL   כתריאל

The Crown of El is the holy place in which I dwell

today. With the Symbolic crown of Knowledge, I

shall follow the intuitive urge to be worthy of the

great gift of all, and the Ability to use the wisdom

in every action.

LAHAVIEL   להביאל

The eternal Flame of EL consuming the ME and

aiding the transformation work I am involved in

at this moment. Fire, the purifying agent, is my gift

today.

MEROMIEL   מרומיאל

The highest place of EL, from where I come, is always

giving me the ability to stay SANE in a world gone mad

from ignorance. I recognize this place to be my place of

transformation, in harmony and in peace.

NETANOUEL   נתנואל

That which is given from EL returns to EL.

Balance of being is my main thought today.

Let me keep this thought constantly in me while

I am, as a reminder of TOTAL BALANCE.

SAHARIEL   סהריאל

The great door of Life coming eternally from

EL is open wide for my entrance to be bathed

with the LIGHT of understanding in all my

thoughts and actions today. I keep myself always

in the LIGHT of EL.

OLAMIEL   עולמיאל

The Universal Power of EL murmuring into my

heart the secret of Silence and Simplicity, of

Harmonious relationship with other universes.

There is no place empty of EL. EL is in me, I am

in EL.

PARDESIEL   פרדסיאל

The Garden of Wisdom of EL is greeting me to explore

the unknown. Its intelligence lives in every particle that

makes this body live. My heart is full of gratitude for

Being in the Garden.

TZIDKATIEL   צדקתיאל

The justice and EL is today's main dwelling thought.

Let me become aware of the injustices I have made

toward all who come in touch with me and be forgiving.

Teach me to SEE with the Just eye of EL.

KOLIEL   קוֹלִיאֵל

The inner voice of EL is calling me to listen to

the sound of silence in which I can distinguish

between the Ego and the intuitive messages. I

am confident to be guided to the answer of the

inner calling.

RAMMUEL   רמהואל

From the HILL of EL, the space of heights

and Oneness of RAM, EL is listening to me.

I ask only to be useful to others and to be

worthy to respond to the "I am" within me,

with RAMUEL's guidance.

SHELOMIEL   שלומיאל

The Peace of EL is now enveloping me and

and caressing me with the blessed perfume

from the Garden of Peace. In this profound

state, I broadcast the Peace to all beings,

visibly and invisibly.

TAMIEL   תמיאל

I am now sitting in a place of TAM of EL.

A pure wind of fresh air is flowing through

me in and out, collecting the energetic

"WIND OF EL" to make me whole and free

from all negativities. TAMIEL is in me, I

am in TAMIEL.

SACRED POEMS

THE RADIANT LETTERS

הָאוֹתִיּוֹת הַזּוֹהֲרוֹת

1. To the midst of the storm that
   penetrates "me,"
   To the center of my
   consciousness, my hidden
   soul whispered,
   She murmured to me in silence
   the secret of existence of the cells
   That are working with faithfulness
   The Great Work of the heart.

א. אֶל תּוֹךְ הַסַּעַר שֶׁחָדַר לְתוֹכִי
אֶל מֶרְכַּז תּוֹדַעְתִּי, רוּחַ נֶעֶלָמָה
לַחֲשָׁה לִי אֶת סוֹד הַקִּיּוּם,
שֶׁל תָּאִים עוֹבְדִים בְּנֶאֱמָנוּת
אֶת הָעֲבוֹדָה הַגְּדוֹלָה שֶׁבַּלֵּב.

2. And like wake/sleep, I reflected in
   the endless space,
   between the eternal forests,
   between the high mountains,
   That hug the majesty of the horizon.
   in which I dwell now.

ב. וּכְמוֹ יָשֵׁן-עֵר הַזֵּיתִי
בְּאוֹתוֹ חָלָל אֵין סוֹפִי, בֵּין
יְעָרוֹת הָעַד, בֵּין הֶהָרִים הַגְּבוֹהִים
הָאוֹמְרוֹת לְחַבֵּק אֶת הָאוֹפֶק הַנִּפְלָא
בּוֹ שׁוֹכֵן אֲנִי עַכְשָׁו

3. And Lo -- The letters with a splendor
   glow
   Dancing before me with mighty light,
   Like seducing me to EAT and
   be satisfied from their bounty
   wisdom.
   And all of me transmuted to be one
   letter and another letter.
   I am the letter,
   I am the letters of LIGHT.

ג. וְהִנֵּה אוֹתִיּוֹת בְּאוֹר זוֹהַר
מְרַקְּדוֹת מוּלִי בְּאוֹר בָּהִיר
כִּמְפַתּוֹת אוֹתִי לֶאֱכוֹל וְלִשְׂבּוֹעַ
מְטוּבָם, וְכוּלִּי הוֹפֵךְ לִהְיוֹת אוֹת
וְעוֹד אוֹת, אֲנִי אוֹת,
אֲנִי אוֹתִיּוֹת הָאוֹר

THE RADIANT LETTERS

הָאוֹתִיּוֹת הַזּוֹהֲרוֹת

4. My eyes hear, my ears see,
    My mouth walks and my hands
        talk the light,
    And I swim in the smooth, great light,
    That unveils and guides me, to the
        WAY TO BE.

ד. עֵינִי שׁוֹמַעַת, אָזְנִי רוֹאָה,
    פִּי הוֹלֵךְ, וְיָדַי מְדַבְּרוֹת אֶת
    הָאוֹר הַזּוֹהֵר, וְכוּלִּי שָׁט
    בִּבְהִירוּת, בָּאוֹר הַגָּדוֹל אֲשֶׁר
    גִּלָּה לִי אֶת הַדֶּרֶךְ ל ה י ו ת.

שמואל בן-אור אביטל
ירושלים אב תשל"ג

August 22, 1973
Samuel Ben-Or Avital

THUS SAITH THE ALEPH

THUS SAITH THE ALEPH

I am an ancient echo
  who beats in the heart-bell
  and awakens the flame to soar
  higher than air,

I am the echo of a message
  unwritten, untold,
Buried in the cell primordial,
  Original,
The Yod that multiplies into
  eternal letters.

I am the echo of a forgotten song.
  An unseen leaf reaching to the sun
  in remembrance of mother-soul
  that generates me to BE who I am

I am a thought that has been
  transformed
  into a dot, into lines, into circles
  into cells, into organs, into heart,
  into brain.
Briefly, my friend, the changing
  thought into this "me," scrambles,
  mixes, computes letters and words
  to the pure white of this paper.

כֹּה אָמְרָה הָאוֹת אָלֶף

אֲנִי בַּת-קוֹל עַתִּיקַת הַיּוֹמִין
הַמְצַלְצֶלֶת בְּפַעֲמוֹן-הַלֵּב
וּמְעוֹרֶרֶת שַׁלְהֶבֶת-אֵל-יָהּ
לְהַרְקִיעַ שְׁחָקִים מֵעֵבֶר לֶחָלָל.

אֲנִי הַבְּשׂוֹרָה הַלֹּא כְּתוּבָה, הַלֹּא נֶאֱמֶרֶת,
הַקְּבוּרָה בִּתְהוֹם הַתָּא הַמְּקוֹרִי
שֶׁל רֵאשִׁית הַבְּרִיאָה.
אֶת הַיּוֹד הַפּוֹרָה וְהַמִּתְרַבֶּה,
הַמַּכְפִּילָה הֲוָיָתָהּ לְאוֹתִיּוֹת אוֹר הַנֶּצַח.

אֲנִי הֵד הַשִּׁיר הַנִּשְׁכַּח,
עָלֶה נֶעֱלָם הַמַּפְלִיג אֶל הַשֶּׁמֶשׁ
לַעֲבוֹר אֶת נִיצוֹץ הַנְּשָׁמָה, אֵם-רֵאשִׁית
שֶׁהוֹלִידָה וּבָרְאָה אוֹתִי
לִהְיוֹת אֶת הַנֶּצַח הַמְהַוֶּה אוֹתִי, מָה שֶׁאֲנִי.

אֲנִי הַמַּחֲשָׁבָה, פּוֹשֶׁטֶת צוּרָה
וְלוֹבֶשֶׁת צוּרָה לַתָּאִים לַנְּקוּדָה, לַקַּוִּים
לָעִיגוּלִים, לָאֵבָרִים, וְלַמּוֹחַ, בְּקִיצוּר יְדִידִי,
הַמַּחֲשָׁבָה הַמִּשְׁתַּנָּה אֶל הָאֲנִי הַזֶּה.
הַמַּרְכִּיב וּמְעַרְבֵּב וּמְצָרֵף אוֹתִיּוֹת וּמִילִים
לְתוֹךְ טוֹהַר הַלּוֹבֶן שֶׁל הַנְּיָר.

THUS SAITH THE ALEPH

I am the place of justice, balance,
   calm and tranquility.

אֲנִי מְקוֹם מִשְׁכָּן הַצֶּדֶק,
הָאִיזּוּן הַשָּׁקוּל, הַשֶּׁלָו וְהַרְגּוּעַ.

I am the time into which all
   beings become.

אֲנִי הַזְּמַן, הָעֵת בּוֹ כָּל יְצוּרֵי-עוֹלָם
מִתְהַוִּים.

I am the light that attracts all
   flames unto me.

אֲנִי הָאוֹר, הַמּוֹשֵׁךְ כָּל אֵשׁ הַלֶּהָבוֹת
אֶל תּוֹכִי.

I am the living word that
   comes through every mouth,
every cell in this eternal
universe.

אֲנִי הַדִּיבֵּר הַחַי הַנֶּאֱמַר מִכָּל פֶּה וְלָשׁוֹן.
וּמִכָּל תָּא וְתָא אֶל עוֹלָם הַנֶּצַח
וְהָאֵין-סוֹף.

Briefly, my friend, I am Thou.

בְּקִיצוּר יְדִידִי, אֲנִי הוּא   הַ אַ תָּ ה.

(Translation by the Author)

מאת : שמואל בן-אור אביטל
חודש אלול תשמ"א
Sept. 1, 1981

Published in <u>AGADA - Hebrew & English</u>
Winter '83, Issue 4, Volume II, No. 1,
Berkeley, California, U.S.A.

THUS SAITH THE BEITH

THUS SAITH THE LETTER BEITH

כֹּה אָמְרָה הָאוֹת בֵּית

Within the BEITH, the bright
blessing of the Creator dwells,
From the utterances of the eternal
covenant, and forever witnessing
to be.

בְּבֵית הַבְּרָכָה הַבְּהִירָה
שׁוֹכֵן הָאֵל הַבּוֹרֵא
וּמִפִּיו בְּרִית הָעַד,
וְעֵדוּת עוֹלָם לִהְיוֹת.

I am the house and the dwelling,
the place of my existence within
point of essence of essences.

אֲנִי בֵּיתוֹ וּמִשְׁכָּנוֹ
בִּי הוּא נָע, בִּי הוּא נָד.
אֶל נְקוּדַת עִיקַר הָעִיקָרִים.

My name is my house, my
understanding and intelligence.
My form is the form of a house
sitting and leaning in the Creator's
trust.

שְׁמִי הוּא בֵּיתִי,
הוּא בִּינָתִי וּתְבוּנָתִי.
צוּרָתִי צוּרַת בֵּית
יוֹשֵׁב וְנִשְׁעַן עַל יְהָבֵי-אֵל.

I contain within me, all living
beginnings. And, my infinite cosmic
container exists within her forever.

אֲנִי מְכִילָה בְּתוֹכִי
כָּל רֵאשִׁית חַי,
וּתְכוּלָתִי הַיְקוּמִית-אֵינְסוֹפִית
תִּתְקַיֵּים לָעַד בָּה.

The nests of the foundation of life
moves and moves always until my
conscious wisdom is contained in all of
creation.

קָנְקַנֵּי יְסוֹדוֹת הַחַיִּים
בִּי בְּתוֹךְ עַצְמִי נָעִים וְזָזִים
עַד אֲשֶׁר תּוֹדַעְתִּי הַחָכְמָה
בְּכָל הַבְּרִיאָה תָּכִיל

THUS SAITH THE LETTER BEITH

כֹּה אָמְרָה הָאוֹת בֵּית

Without my dwelling, there is no
spatial stability. As it was, as it
is, and as it will be in my frontiers
and my dwelling, there will
you find eternal rest.

בִּלְעֲדֵי בֵּיתִי אֵין יַצִּיבוּת בֶּחָלָל,
הוּא הָיָה, הוּא הֹוֶה וְהוּא יִהְיֶה
בִּגְבוּלִי וּמְעוֹנִי
שָׁם יִמָּצֵא מְנוּחַת עוֹלָם.

His dwelling and her dwelling is
my dwelling. His place and her
place is my place. The beginning and
the end is within me. The Creator's
name will endure.

מִשְׁכָּנוֹ וּמִשְׁכָּנָה מִשְׁכָּנִי,
וּמְקוֹמוֹ מְקוֹמָה מְקוֹמִי
הָרֵאשִׁית וְהָאַחֲרִית
בִּי יְקוּיִּים שֵׁם הַבּוֹרֵא.

The chaos and the blessing in me
are one. His flesh and her flesh
is my flesh. Visible and invisible.

הַבֹּהוּ וְהַבְּרָכָה
חַד הֵם בִּי.
בְּשָׂרוֹ וּבְשָׂרָה בְּשָׂרִי
נִרְאֶה וְלֹא נִרְאֶה.

In the site of my existence and my
being, I will give life until eternity.

בַּאֲתַר הֱיוֹתִי וְקִיּוּמִי
אֶתֵּן אֶת הַחַיִּים עַד עוֹלָם.

שמואל בן-אור אביטל
י"ב אלול תשמ"א - Sept. 11, 1981

310

THE COSMIC ACCORDION

COSMIC ACCORDION

This expression, "Cosmic Accordion," was born out of necessity. Over the years, in working with my students, I found this natural law occurring over and over again in many and varied situations. But it had no name. We explored it together, and after some time it finally distilled itself into these two words which, as part of our vocabulary of condensed communication, shortens the space between thought and action in our actual class sessions. Thus, we are able to talk about it, to see it, to reflect upon it, to BE it.

The Cosmic Accordion is the journey between the infinitely small and the infinitely big, back and forth and back again. This process is inherent in the study of any art. By going deeply into the creative process and deeply into the self, one will eventually come upon the source of creativity -- a source which is infinitely vast.

The artistic process begins with the artist's talent. Added to this, is that which we call "inspiration" and what then remains is to manifest it, actualize it, physicalize it. This is the artist's or the mystic's real work. Once the source of inspiration has been tapped, (the infinitely large), the challenge is to bring it "down to earth," to materialize the realization for others to see, hear or feel so that it might be appreciate and communicated.

This funneling is called, in Hebrew, TZIMTZUM (צמצום) or condensation. The artist, or the mystic, becomes the vehicle, vessel, channel through which the infinitely big (inspiration) is poured and gets molded by the artist's masterly actions. This renders it visible, audible or tactile as the case may be. In mime, it is the process of visibilizing the invisible.

For the mime, the body itself is the vessel. It shapes and forms gesture, rhythm, and attitude, manifesting that which is invisible and infinite. The mime must BECOME that which he wishes to render. He is the medium itself, as well as its creator. He is the color, the musicality. He is the very thought made manifest.

In the actual exchange between artist and audience, the artist hopes to re-create the experience of the infinitely large so that it can be passed on to those who are sharing or participating in the creation. When the audience receives it in its condensed physicalized, manifested form, it goes into the unconscious as an experience or perception, and is, thus, returned to its source. It has become, once again, infinitely vast. Thus, the circle is complete.

This same Cosmic Accordion is active constantly in the spiritual quest. In meditation and divine contemplation, we wish to experience, even for a brief moment, the freedom from the body and its physical limits. In these moments, there is often an experience of being a part of the vast cosmic ocean. We are a mere speck -- infinitely small in the cosmic scheme -- but when we merge with this ocean, we feel that we have BECOME IT in all its vastness.

On the spiritual path, one learns to look within the self for many answers and to find all the expressions of the universe represented within the limits of the human body. There is a continual interplay between the large and the small. One is like a pendulum, swinging back and forth between the opposites ever seeking to find the balance, the middle pillar, where one can be in both "places" at once. One encounters here the paradox of that which is apparently insignificant on the one hand, but, is tremendously significant on the other. All the great teachers throughout the course of history have presented their wisdom in this way -- condensing, from the greater vision, their spiritual knowledge into the material world.

For the Kabbalist, the Cosmic Accordion is a ubiquitous principle, many variations of which can be found in every corner of the Kabblistic literature. In one instance, it can be seen as the journey downward through the spectrum of the four worlds -- Atzilut (אצילות), the world of emanation; Beriya (בריאה), the world of creation; Yetzira (יצירה),

315

the world of formation; Assiya (עשיה), the world of making of matter.

Through "inspiration," one may be graced with the ability to pull the idea from the world of Atzilut (the upper, big triangle) down through the world of creation and the world of formation into the world of making. In other words, it is the process of creation itself, or the formula for bringing that which is hidden into the manifest world, from the invisible to the visible. This process allows for the possibility of communicating that specific idea or concept, for making manifest in the physical world that which is ordinarily inaccessible by usual means.

This experiential concept is also used by the Kabbalists to interpret the Ladder of Jacob. In this case, it is the "angels" which descend, ascend, back and forth in the eternal vertical process of manifesting the God within. It is a participation in the great plan or scheme of human evolution from matter to spirit, form spirit to matter; the grand cosmic theatre created to "entertain" the angels, humans, animals and all the kingdoms through which the Great One, the unnameable, manifests Him self.

THE LAST WORD

THE LAST WORD

In the hope that this gathering of thoughts are an assistance for your study and reflection, this little assembly of letters and words were written with the intention of "revealing" what is "hidden."

To see that which is so obvious and very near to us, one needs only to expand the awareness, to look beneath and deeply beyond all appearances. In this "hidden" realm, one must deal with the world of the images of the Creator and the true reality of the awakened ones, the sages, who, in their anonymity and enlightenment, have paved the magnificent path to the Science of the Holy Kabbalah.

The ancient tradition of using words in a certain way to stimulate and deepen our understanding of the universe and the laws that govern it, and of acting accordingly in harmony with all that is, is what I call the "the holiness of being ordinary."

It is with this in mind that this little book is offered for the benefit of all, so that we might find, by sharing the same breath together, the near-ness in the far-ness, the order in the chaos, the calm within the tumult. It is offered with the prayer that we may find our own note of Cosmic music from which to function as awakened cells inside this human organism; to fulfill our mission and work for the benefit of mankind; to serve in

Sacred Silence. Living in our perplexed times of separation and strife, we must manifest the unity in all in order to heal that which is inharmonious and out of tune. How? -- By knowing, simply, our own place in the scheme of life, thus balancing the energies in our "being of light" and serving better the Creator's plan with excellence and impeccability.

I seal these words with an ancient prayer given to me when I was a child:

"CREATOR OF THE UNIVERSE, KEEP ME SANE IN THE MIST OF MADNESS."

So be it, and may Profound Peace be with you and all Creation.

From a Friend of Humanity.

*Workshop Event: *Dynamic Movement of the Hebrew Letters*

This workshop event **(22 weekends)**, is an introduction to developing with the participants a series of **Aleph Beith Bio-Dynamic movement exercises,** where each letter comes alive, energetically moving, expressing itself with the whole body and soul.

Through the kinesthetic awareness of the Hebrew letters, we explore ourselves and our relationship to ourselves and the "other," and to the inner and outer meaning of the Hebrew letters and the Hebrew language.

The workshop of the Hebrew Letters is by invitation only. Please inquire at Le Centre du Silence, Boulder, Colorado, USA. See the article, **"A Dot in Space"** in the *Mime Workbook*, by Samuel Avital.

Samuel Ben-Or Avital conducts special workshops to introduce the **Dynamic Movement of the Hebrew Letters**, the Cosmic and Inner profound meaning of the Hebrew letters, by learning to embody the knowledge and the Code of the Sacred Letters through experience, rather than just understanding the letters intellectually and mentally.

GENESIS
(Appendix A)

ספר בראשית

THE BOOK OF GENESIS.

בראשית

CHAPTER I.

IN the beginning God created the heaven and
the earth.

2 And the earth was without form, and void;
and darkness *was* upon the face of the deep.
And the spirit of God moved upon the face of
the waters.

3 And God said, Let there be light: and
there was light.

4 And God saw the light, that *it was* good:
and God divided the light from the darkness.

5 And God called the light Day, and the
darkness he called Night. And the evening and
the morning were the first day.

6 And God said, Let there be a firmament
in the midst of the waters, and let it divide the
waters from the waters.

7 And God made the firmament, and divided
the waters which *were* under the firmament from
the waters which *were* above the firmament: and
it was so.

8 And God called the firmament Heaven. And
the evening and the morning were the second
day.

9 And God said, Let the waters under
the heaven be gathered together unto one
place, and let the dry *land* appear: and it
was so.

10 And God called the dry *land* Earth; and
the gathering together of the waters called he
Seas: and God saw that *it was* good.

11 And God said, Let the earth bring forth
grass, the herb yielding seed, *and* the fruit tree
yielding fruit after his kind, whose seed *is* in
itself, upon the earth: and it was so.

בְּרֵאשִׁ֖ית בָּרָ֣א אֱלֹהִ֑ים אֵ֥ת הַשָּׁמַ֖יִם וְאֵ֥ת 1
הָאָֽרֶץ: וְהָאָ֗רֶץ הָיְתָ֥ה תֹ֙הוּ֙ וָבֹ֔הוּ וְחֹ֖שֶׁךְ 2
עַל־פְּנֵ֣י תְה֑וֹם וְר֣וּחַ אֱלֹהִ֔ים מְרַחֶ֖פֶת עַל־
פְּנֵ֥י הַמָּֽיִם: וַיֹּ֥אמֶר אֱלֹהִ֖ים יְהִ֣י א֑וֹר 3
וַֽיְהִי־אֽוֹר: וַיַּ֧רְא אֱלֹהִ֛ים אֶת־הָא֖וֹר 4
כִּי־ט֑וֹב וַיַּבְדֵּ֣ל אֱלֹהִ֔ים בֵּ֥ין הָא֖וֹר וּבֵ֥ין
הַחֹֽשֶׁךְ: וַיִּקְרָ֨א אֱלֹהִ֤ים ׀ לָאוֹר֙ י֔וֹם 5
וְלַחֹ֖שֶׁךְ קָ֣רָא לָ֑יְלָה וַֽיְהִי־עֶ֥רֶב וַֽיְהִי־בֹ֖קֶר
י֥וֹם אֶחָֽד: פ

וַיֹּ֣אמֶר אֱלֹהִ֔ים יְהִ֥י רָקִ֖יעַ בְּת֣וֹךְ הַמָּ֑יִם 6
וִיהִ֣י מַבְדִּ֔יל בֵּ֥ין מַ֖יִם לָמָֽיִם: וַיַּ֣עַשׂ 7
אֱלֹהִים֮ אֶת־הָרָקִיעַ֒ וַיַּבְדֵּ֗ל בֵּ֤ין הַמַּ֙יִם֙
אֲשֶׁר֙ מִתַּ֣חַת לָרָקִ֔יעַ וּבֵ֣ין הַמַּ֔יִם אֲשֶׁ֖ר
מֵעַ֣ל לָרָקִ֑יעַ וַֽיְהִי־כֵֽן: וַיִּקְרָ֧א אֱלֹהִ֛ים 8
לָֽרָקִ֖יעַ שָׁמָ֑יִם וַֽיְהִי־עֶ֥רֶב וַֽיְהִי־בֹ֖קֶר י֥וֹם
שֵׁנִֽי: פ

וַיֹּ֣אמֶר אֱלֹהִ֗ים יִקָּו֨וּ הַמַּ֜יִם מִתַּ֤חַת הַשָּׁמַ֙יִם֙ 9
אֶל־מָק֣וֹם אֶחָ֔ד וְתֵרָאֶ֖ה הַיַּבָּשָׁ֑ה וַֽיְהִי־כֵֽן:
וַיִּקְרָ֨א אֱלֹהִ֤ים ׀ לַיַּבָּשָׁה֙ אֶ֔רֶץ וּלְמִקְוֵ֥ה הַמַּ֖יִם 10
קָרָ֣א יַמִּ֑ים וַיַּ֥רְא אֱלֹהִ֖ים כִּי־טֽוֹב: וַיֹּ֣אמֶר 11
אֱלֹהִ֗ים תַּֽדְשֵׁ֤א הָאָ֙רֶץ֙ דֶּ֔שֶׁא עֵ֚שֶׂב מַזְרִ֣יעַ
זֶ֔רַע עֵ֣ץ פְּרִ֞י עֹ֤שֶׂה פְּרִי֙ לְמִינ֔וֹ אֲשֶׁ֥ר זַרְעוֹ־
ב֖וֹ עַל־הָאָ֑רֶץ וַֽיְהִי־כֵֽן: וַתּוֹצֵ֨א הָאָ֜רֶץ 12

ב׳ רבתי 1 .v

12 And the earth brought forth grass, *and* herb yielding seed after his kind, and the tree yielding fruit, whose seed *was* in itself, after his kind: and God saw that *it was* good.

13 And the evening and the morning were the third day.

14 And God said, Let there be lights in the firmament of the heaven to divide the day from the night; and let them be for signs, and for seasons, and for days, and years:

15 And let them be for lights in the firmament of the heaven to give light upon the earth: and it was so.

16 And God made two great lights; the greater light to rule the day, and the lesser light to rule the night: *he made* the stars also.

17 And God set them in the firmament of the heaven to give light upon the earth,

18 And to rule over the day and over the night, and to divide the light from the darkness: and God saw that *it was* good.

19 And the evening and the morning were the fourth day.

20 And God said, Let the waters bring forth abundantly the moving creature that hath life, and fowl *that* may fly above the earth in the open firmament of heaven.

21 And God created great whales, and every living creature that moveth which the waters brought forth abundantly, after their kind, and every winged fowl after his kind: and God saw that *it was* good.

22 And God blessed them, saying, Be fruitful, and multiply, and fill the waters in the seas, and let fowl multiply in the earth.

23 And the evening and the morning were the fifth day.

24 And God said, Let the earth bring forth the living creature after his kind, cattle, and creeping thing, and beast of the earth after his kind: and it was so.

25 And God made the beast of the earth after his kind, and cattle after their kind, and every thing that creepeth upon the earth after his kind: and God saw that *it was* good.

26 And God said, Let us make man in our image, after our likeness: and let them have dominion over the fish of the sea, and over the fowl of the air, and over the cattle, and over all

וַתּוֹצֵא הָאָרֶץ דֶּשֶׁא עֵשֶׂב מַזְרִיעַ זֶרַע לְמִינֵהוּ וְעֵץ עֹשֶׂה־
פְּרִי אֲשֶׁר זַרְעוֹ־בוֹ לְמִינֵהוּ וַיַּרְא אֱלֹהִים
13 כִּי־טוֹב:　　וַיְהִי־עֶרֶב וַיְהִי־בֹקֶר יוֹם
שְׁלִישִׁי: פ　　שני

14 וַיֹּאמֶר אֱלֹהִים יְהִי מְאֹרֹת בִּרְקִיעַ הַשָּׁמַיִם
לְהַבְדִּיל בֵּין הַיּוֹם וּבֵין הַלָּיְלָה וְהָיוּ לְאֹתֹת
15 וּלְמוֹעֲדִים וּלְיָמִים וְשָׁנִים: וְהָיוּ לִמְאוֹרֹת
בִּרְקִיעַ הַשָּׁמַיִם לְהָאִיר עַל־הָאָרֶץ וַיְהִי־כֵן:
16 וַיַּעַשׂ אֱלֹהִים אֶת־שְׁנֵי הַמְּאֹרֹת הַגְּדֹלִים
אֶת־הַמָּאוֹר הַגָּדֹל לְמֶמְשֶׁלֶת הַיּוֹם וְאֶת־
הַמָּאוֹר הַקָּטֹן לְמֶמְשֶׁלֶת הַלַּיְלָה וְאֵת
17 הַכּוֹכָבִים: וַיִּתֵּן אֹתָם אֱלֹהִים בִּרְקִיעַ
18 הַשָּׁמָיִם לְהָאִיר עַל־הָאָרֶץ: וְלִמְשֹׁל בַּיּוֹם
וּבַלַּיְלָה וּלְהַבְדִּיל בֵּין הָאוֹר וּבֵין הַחֹשֶׁךְ
19 וַיַּרְא אֱלֹהִים כִּי־טוֹב: וַיְהִי־עֶרֶב וַיְהִי־בֹקֶר
יוֹם רְבִיעִי: פ

20 וַיֹּאמֶר אֱלֹהִים יִשְׁרְצוּ הַמַּיִם שֶׁרֶץ נֶפֶשׁ
חַיָּה וְעוֹף יְעוֹפֵף עַל־הָאָרֶץ עַל־פְּנֵי רְקִיעַ
21 הַשָּׁמָיִם: וַיִּבְרָא אֱלֹהִים אֶת־הַתַּנִּינִם
הַגְּדֹלִים וְאֵת כָּל־נֶפֶשׁ הַחַיָּה ׀ הָרֹמֶשֶׂת
אֲשֶׁר שָׁרְצוּ הַמַּיִם לְמִינֵהֶם וְאֵת כָּל־עוֹף
22 כָּנָף לְמִינֵהוּ וַיַּרְא אֱלֹהִים כִּי־טוֹב: וַיְבָרֶךְ
אֹתָם אֱלֹהִים לֵאמֹר פְּרוּ וּרְבוּ וּמִלְאוּ אֶת־
23 הַמַּיִם בַּיַּמִּים וְהָעוֹף יִרֶב בָּאָרֶץ: וַיְהִי־עֶרֶב
וַיְהִי־בֹקֶר יוֹם חֲמִישִׁי: פ　　שלישי

24 וַיֹּאמֶר אֱלֹהִים תּוֹצֵא הָאָרֶץ נֶפֶשׁ חַיָּה
לְמִינָהּ בְּהֵמָה וָרֶמֶשׂ וְחַיְתוֹ־אֶרֶץ לְמִינָהּ
25 וַיְהִי־כֵן: וַיַּעַשׂ אֱלֹהִים אֶת־חַיַּת הָאָרֶץ
לְמִינָהּ וְאֶת־הַבְּהֵמָה לְמִינָהּ וְאֵת כָּל־רֶמֶשׂ
הָאֲדָמָה לְמִינֵהוּ וַיַּרְא אֱלֹהִים כִּי־טוֹב:
26 וַיֹּאמֶר אֱלֹהִים נַעֲשֶׂה אָדָם בְּצַלְמֵנוּ
כִּדְמוּתֵנוּ וְיִרְדּוּ בִדְגַת הַיָּם וּבְעוֹף הַשָּׁמַיִם

the earth, and over every creeping thing that creepeth upon the earth.

27 So God created man in his *own* image, in the image of God created he him; male and female created he them.

28 And God blessed them, and God said unto them, Be fruitful, and multiply, and replenish the earth, and subdue it: and have dominion over the fish of the sea, and over the fowl of the air, and over every living thing that moveth upon the earth.

29 And God said, Behold, I have given you every herb bearing seed, which *is* upon the face of all the earth, and every tree, in the which *is* the fruit of a tree yielding seed; to you it shall be for meat.

30 And to every beast of the earth, and to every fowl of the air, and to every thing that creepeth upon the earth, wherein *there is* life, *I have given* every green herb for meat: and it was so.

31 And God saw every thing that he had made, and, behold, *it was* very good. And the evening and the morning were the sixth day

CHAPTER II.

THUS the heavens and the earth were finished, and all the host of them.

2 And on the seventh day God ended his work which he had made; and he rested on the seventh day from all his work which he had made.

3 And God blessed the seventh day, and sanctified it: because that in it he had rested from all his work which God created and made.

4 These *are* the generations of the heavens and of the earth when they were created, in the day that the LORD God made the earth and the heavens,

5 And every plant of the field before it was in the earth, and every herb of the field before it grew: for the LORD God had not caused it to rain upon the earth, and *there was* not a man to till the ground.

6 But there went up a mist from the earth, and watered the whole face of the ground.

7 And the LORD God formed man *of* the dust of the ground, and breathed into his nostrils the breath of life; and man became a living soul.

8 And the LORD God planted a garden eastward in Eden; and there he put the man whom he had formed.

וּבַבְּהֵמָה וּבְכָל־הָאָרֶץ וּבְכָל־הָרֶמֶשׂ הָרֹמֵשׂ
עַל־הָאָרֶץ: וַיִּבְרָא אֱלֹהִים ׀ אֶת־הָאָדָם
בְּצַלְמוֹ בְּצֶלֶם אֱלֹהִים בָּרָא אֹתוֹ זָכָר וּנְקֵבָה
בָּרָא אֹתָם: וַיְבָרֶךְ אֹתָם אֱלֹהִים וַיֹּאמֶר
לָהֶם אֱלֹהִים פְּרוּ וּרְבוּ וּמִלְאוּ אֶת־הָאָרֶץ
וְכִבְשֻׁהָ וּרְדוּ בִּדְגַת הַיָּם וּבְעוֹף הַשָּׁמַיִם
וּבְכָל־חַיָּה הָרֹמֶשֶׂת עַל־הָאָרֶץ: וַיֹּאמֶר
אֱלֹהִים הִנֵּה נָתַתִּי לָכֶם אֶת־כָּל־עֵשֶׂב ׀ זֹרֵעַ
זֶרַע אֲשֶׁר עַל־פְּנֵי כָל־הָאָרֶץ וְאֶת־כָּל־
הָעֵץ אֲשֶׁר־בּוֹ פְרִי־עֵץ זֹרֵעַ זָרַע לָכֶם יִהְיֶה
לְאָכְלָה: וּלְכָל־חַיַּת הָאָרֶץ וּלְכָל־עוֹף
הַשָּׁמַיִם וּלְכֹל ׀ רוֹמֵשׂ עַל־הָאָרֶץ אֲשֶׁר־בּוֹ
נֶפֶשׁ חַיָּה אֶת־כָּל־יֶרֶק עֵשֶׂב לְאָכְלָה וַיְהִי־
כֵן: וַיַּרְא אֱלֹהִים אֶת־כָּל־אֲשֶׁר עָשָׂה
וְהִנֵּה־טוֹב מְאֹד וַיְהִי־עֶרֶב וַיְהִי־בֹקֶר יוֹם
הַשִּׁשִּׁי: פ

וַיְכֻלּוּ הַשָּׁמַיִם וְהָאָרֶץ וְכָל־צְבָאָם: וַיְכַל
אֱלֹהִים בַּיּוֹם הַשְּׁבִיעִי מְלַאכְתּוֹ אֲשֶׁר עָשָׂה
וַיִּשְׁבֹּת בַּיּוֹם הַשְּׁבִיעִי מִכָּל־מְלַאכְתּוֹ אֲשֶׁר
עָשָׂה: וַיְבָרֶךְ אֱלֹהִים אֶת־יוֹם הַשְּׁבִיעִי
וַיְקַדֵּשׁ אֹתוֹ כִּי בוֹ שָׁבַת מִכָּל־מְלַאכְתּוֹ
אֲשֶׁר־בָּרָא אֱלֹהִים לַעֲשׂוֹת: פ רביעי
אֵלֶּה תוֹלְדוֹת הַשָּׁמַיִם וְהָאָרֶץ בְּהִבָּרְאָם
בְּיוֹם עֲשׂוֹת יְהוָה אֱלֹהִים אֶרֶץ וְשָׁמָיִם:
וְכֹל ׀ שִׂיחַ הַשָּׂדֶה טֶרֶם יִהְיֶה בָאָרֶץ וְכָל־
עֵשֶׂב הַשָּׂדֶה טֶרֶם יִצְמָח כִּי לֹא הִמְטִיר
יְהוָה אֱלֹהִים עַל־הָאָרֶץ וְאָדָם אַיִן לַעֲבֹד
אֶת־הָאֲדָמָה: וְאֵד יַעֲלֶה מִן־הָאָרֶץ וְהִשְׁקָה
אֶת־כָּל־פְּנֵי הָאֲדָמָה: וַיִּיצֶר יְהוָה אֱלֹהִים
אֶת־הָאָדָם עָפָר מִן־הָאֲדָמָה וַיִּפַּח בְּאַפָּיו
נִשְׁמַת חַיִּים וַיְהִי הָאָדָם לְנֶפֶשׁ חַיָּה: וַיִּטַּע
יְהוָה אֱלֹהִים גַּן בְּעֵדֶן מִקֶּדֶם וַיָּשֶׂם שָׁם אֶת־

327

9 And out of the ground made the LORD God to grow every tree that is pleasant to the sight, and good for food ; the tree of life also in the midst of the garden, and the tree of knowledge of good and evil.

10 And a river went out of Eden to water the garden ; and from thence it was parted, and became into four heads.

11 The name of the first is Pison : that is it which compasseth the whole land of Havilah, where there is gold ;

12 And the gold of that land is good : there is bdellium and the onyx stone.

13 And the name of the second river is Gihon : the same is it that compasseth the whole land of Ethiopia.

14 And the name of the third river is Hiddekel : that is it which goeth toward the east of Assyria. And the fourth river is Euphrates.

15 And the LORD God took the man, and put him into the garden of Eden to dress it and to keep it.

16 And the LORD God commanded the man, saying, Of every tree of the garden thou mayest freely eat :

17 But of the tree of the knowledge of good and evil, thou shalt not eat of it : for in the day that thou eatest thereof thou shalt surely die.

18 And the LORD God said, It is not good that the man should be alone ; I will make him an help meet for him.

19 And out of the ground the LORD God formed every beast of the field, and every fowl of the air ; and brought them unto Adam to see what he would call them : and whatsoever Adam called every living creature, that was the name thereof.

20 And Adam gave names to all cattle, and to the fowl of the air, and to every beast of the field ; but for Adam there was not found an help meet for him.

21 And the LORD God caused a deep sleep to fall upon Adam, and he slept : and he took one of his ribs, and closed up the flesh instead thereof ;

22 And the rib, which the LORD God had taken from man, made he a woman, and brought her unto the man.

23 And Adam said, This is now bone of my bones, and flesh of my flesh : she shall be called Woman, because she was taken out of Man.

24 Therefore shall a man leave his father and his mother, and shall cleave unto his wife : and they shall be one flesh.

25 And they were both naked, the man and

הָאָדָם אֲשֶׁר יָצָר: וַיַּצְמַח יְהֹוָה אֱלֹהִים 9
מִן־הָאֲדָמָה כָּל־עֵץ נֶחְמָד לְמַרְאֶה וְטוֹב
לְמַאֲכָל וְעֵץ הַחַיִּים בְּתוֹךְ הַגָּן וְעֵץ הַדַּעַת
טוֹב וָרָע: וְנָהָר יֹצֵא מֵעֵדֶן לְהַשְׁקוֹת אֶת־ 10
הַגָּן וּמִשָּׁם יִפָּרֵד וְהָיָה לְאַרְבָּעָה רָאשִׁים:
שֵׁם הָאֶחָד פִּישׁוֹן הוּא הַסֹּבֵב אֵת כָּל־אֶרֶץ 11
הַחֲוִילָה אֲשֶׁר־שָׁם הַזָּהָב: וּזֲהַב הָאָרֶץ 12
הַהִוא טוֹב שָׁם הַבְּדֹלַח וְאֶבֶן הַשֹּׁהַם: וְשֵׁם־ 13
הַנָּהָר הַשֵּׁנִי גִּיחוֹן הוּא הַסּוֹבֵב אֵת כָּל־אֶרֶץ
כּוּשׁ: וְשֵׁם הַנָּהָר הַשְּׁלִישִׁי חִדֶּקֶל הוּא 14
הַהֹלֵךְ קִדְמַת אַשּׁוּר וְהַנָּהָר הָרְבִיעִי הוּא
פְרָת: וַיִּקַּח יְהֹוָה אֱלֹהִים אֶת־הָאָדָם וַיַּנִּחֵהוּ 15
בְגַן־עֵדֶן לְעָבְדָהּ וּלְשָׁמְרָהּ: וַיְצַו יְהֹוָה 16
אֱלֹהִים עַל־הָאָדָם לֵאמֹר מִכֹּל עֵץ־הַגָּן
אָכֹל תֹּאכֵל: וּמֵעֵץ הַדַּעַת טוֹב וָרָע לֹא 17
תֹאכַל מִמֶּנּוּ כִּי בְּיוֹם אֲכָלְךָ מִמֶּנּוּ מוֹת
תָּמוּת: וַיֹּאמֶר יְהֹוָה אֱלֹהִים לֹא־טוֹב הֱיוֹת 18
הָאָדָם לְבַדּוֹ אֶעֱשֶׂה־לּוֹ עֵזֶר כְּנֶגְדּוֹ: וַיִּצֶר 19
יְהֹוָה אֱלֹהִים מִן־הָאֲדָמָה כָּל־חַיַּת הַשָּׂדֶה
וְאֵת כָּל־עוֹף הַשָּׁמַיִם וַיָּבֵא אֶל־הָאָדָם
לִרְאוֹת מַה־יִּקְרָא־לוֹ וְכֹל אֲשֶׁר יִקְרָא־לוֹ
הָאָדָם נֶפֶשׁ חַיָּה הוּא שְׁמוֹ: וַיִּקְרָא הָאָדָם 20
שֵׁמוֹת לְכָל־הַבְּהֵמָה וּלְעוֹף הַשָּׁמַיִם וּלְכֹל
חַיַּת הַשָּׂדֶה וּלְאָדָם לֹא־מָצָא עֵזֶר כְּנֶגְדּוֹ:
וַיַּפֵּל יְהֹוָה אֱלֹהִים ׀ תַּרְדֵּמָה עַל־הָאָדָם וַיִּישָׁן 21
וַיִּקַּח אַחַת מִצַּלְעֹתָיו וַיִּסְגֹּר בָּשָׂר תַּחְתֶּנָּה:
וַיִּבֶן יְהֹוָה אֱלֹהִים ׀ אֶת־הַצֵּלָע אֲשֶׁר־לָקַח 22
מִן־הָאָדָם לְאִשָּׁה וַיְבִאֶהָ אֶל־הָאָדָם:
וַיֹּאמֶר הָאָדָם זֹאת הַפַּעַם עֶצֶם מֵעֲצָמַי וּבָשָׂר 23
מִבְּשָׂרִי לְזֹאת יִקָּרֵא אִשָּׁה כִּי מֵאִישׁ לֻקֳחָה־
זֹּאת: עַל־כֵּן יַעֲזָב־אִישׁ אֶת־אָבִיו וְאֶת־אִמּוֹ 24
וְדָבַק בְּאִשְׁתּוֹ וְהָיוּ לְבָשָׂר אֶחָד: וַיִּהְיוּ 25

his wife, and were not ashamed.

CHAPTER III.

NOW the serpent was more subtil than any beast of the field which the Lord God had made. And he said unto the woman, Yea, hath God said, Ye shall not eat of every tree of the garden?

2 And the woman said unto the serpent, We may eat of the fruit of the trees of the garden:

3 But of the fruit of the tree which is in the midst of the garden, God hath said, Ye shall not eat of it, neither shall ye touch it, lest ye die.

4 And the serpent said unto the woman, Ye shall not surely die:

5 For God doth know that in the day ye eat thereof, then your eyes shall be opened, and ye shall be as gods, knowing good and evil.

6 And when the woman saw that the tree was good for food, and that it was pleasant to the eyes, and a tree to be desired to make one wise, she took of the fruit thereof, and did eat, and gave also unto her husband with her; and he did eat.

7 And the eyes of them both were opened, and they knew that they were naked; and they sewed fig leaves together, and made themselves aprons.

8 And they heard the voice of the Lord God walking in the garden in the cool of the day: and Adam and his wife hid themselves from the presence of the Lord God amongst the trees of the garden.

9 And the Lord God called unto Adam, and said unto him, Where art thou?

10 And he said, I heard thy voice in the garden, and I was afraid, because I was naked; and I hid myself.

11 And he said, Who told thee that thou wast naked? Hast thou eaten of the tree, whereof I commanded thee that thou shouldest not eat?

12 And the man said, The woman whom thou gavest to be with me, she gave me of the tree, and I did eat.

13 And the Lord God said unto the woman, What is this that thou hast done? And the woman said, The serpent beguiled me, and I did eat.

14 And the Lord God said unto the serpent, Because thou hast done this, thou art cursed above all cattle, and above every beast of the field; upon thy belly shalt thou go, and dust shalt thou eat all the days of thy life:

15 And I will put enmity between thee and the woman, and between thy seed and her seed;

שְׁנֵיהֶם עֲרוּמִּים הָאָדָם וְאִשְׁתּוֹ וְלֹא
יִתְבּשָׁשׁוּ׃

וְהַנָּחָשׁ הָיָה עָרוּם מִכֹּל חַיַּת הַשָּׂדֶה אֲשֶׁר
עָשָׂה יְהֹוָה אֱלֹהִים וַיֹּאמֶר אֶל־הָאִשָּׁה אַף
כִּי־אָמַר אֱלֹהִים לֹא תֹאכְלוּ מִכֹּל עֵץ הַגָּן׃

2 וַתֹּאמֶר הָאִשָּׁה אֶל־הַנָּחָשׁ מִפְּרִי עֵץ־הַגָּן
3 נֹאכֵל׃ וּמִפְּרִי הָעֵץ אֲשֶׁר בְּתוֹךְ־הַגָּן אָמַר
אֱלֹהִים לֹא תֹאכְלוּ מִמֶּנּוּ וְלֹא תִגְּעוּ בּוֹ פֶּן־
4 תְּמֻתוּן׃ וַיֹּאמֶר הַנָּחָשׁ אֶל־הָאִשָּׁה לֹא־מוֹת
5 תְּמֻתוּן׃ כִּי יֹדֵעַ אֱלֹהִים כִּי בְּיוֹם אֲכָלְכֶם
מִמֶּנּוּ וְנִפְקְחוּ עֵינֵיכֶם וִהְיִיתֶם כֵּאלֹהִים יֹדְעֵי
6 טוֹב וָרָע׃ וַתֵּרֶא הָאִשָּׁה כִּי טוֹב הָעֵץ
לְמַאֲכָל וְכִי תַאֲוָה־הוּא לָעֵינַיִם וְנֶחְמָד הָעֵץ
לְהַשְׂכִּיל וַתִּקַּח מִפִּרְיוֹ וַתֹּאכַל וַתִּתֵּן גַּם־
7 לְאִישָׁהּ עִמָּהּ וַיֹּאכַל׃ וַתִּפָּקַחְנָה עֵינֵי שְׁנֵיהֶם
וַיֵּדְעוּ כִּי עֵירֻמִּם הֵם וַיִּתְפְּרוּ עֲלֵה תְאֵנָה
8 וַיַּעֲשׂוּ לָהֶם חֲגֹרֹת׃ וַיִּשְׁמְעוּ אֶת־קוֹל יְהֹוָה
אֱלֹהִים מִתְהַלֵּךְ בַּגָּן לְרוּחַ הַיּוֹם וַיִּתְחַבֵּא
הָאָדָם וְאִשְׁתּוֹ מִפְּנֵי יְהֹוָה אֱלֹהִים בְּתוֹךְ עֵץ
9 הַגָּן׃ וַיִּקְרָא יְהֹוָה אֱלֹהִים אֶל־הָאָדָם וַיֹּאמֶר
10 לוֹ אַיֶּכָּה׃ וַיֹּאמֶר אֶת־קֹלְךָ שָׁמַעְתִּי בַּגָּן
וָאִירָא כִּי־עֵירֹם אָנֹכִי וָאֵחָבֵא׃ וַיֹּאמֶר מִי
11 הִגִּיד לְךָ כִּי עֵירֹם אָתָּה הֲמִן־הָעֵץ אֲשֶׁר
12 צִוִּיתִיךָ לְבִלְתִּי אֲכָל־מִמֶּנּוּ אָכָלְתָּ׃ וַיֹּאמֶר
הָאָדָם הָאִשָּׁה אֲשֶׁר נָתַתָּה עִמָּדִי הִוא
13 נָתְנָה־לִּי מִן־הָעֵץ וָאֹכֵל׃ וַיֹּאמֶר יְהֹוָה
אֱלֹהִים לָאִשָּׁה מַה־זֹּאת עָשִׂית וַתֹּאמֶר
14 הָאִשָּׁה הַנָּחָשׁ הִשִּׁיאַנִי וָאֹכֵל׃ וַיֹּאמֶר יְהֹוָה
אֱלֹהִים אֶל־הַנָּחָשׁ כִּי עָשִׂיתָ זֹּאת אָרוּר
אַתָּה מִכָּל־הַבְּהֵמָה וּמִכֹּל חַיַּת הַשָּׂדֶה עַל־
גְּחֹנְךָ תֵלֵךְ וְעָפָר תֹּאכַל כָּל־יְמֵי חַיֶּיךָ׃
15 וְאֵיבָה אָשִׁית בֵּינְךָ וּבֵין הָאִשָּׁה וּבֵין זַרְעֲךָ

it shall bruise thy head, and thou shalt bruise his heel.

16 Unto the woman he said, I will greatly multiply thy sorrow and thy conception; in sorrow thou shalt bring forth children; and thy desire *shall be* to thy husband, and he shall rule over thee.

17 And unto Adam he said, Because thou hast hearkened unto the voice of thy wife, and hast eaten of the tree, of which I commanded thee, saying, Thou shalt not eat of it: cursed *is* the ground for thy sake; in sorrow shalt thou eat *of* it all the days of thy life;

18 Thorns also and thistles shall it bring forth to thee; and thou shalt eat the herb of the field;

19 In the sweat of thy face shalt thou eat bread, till thou return unto the ground; for out of it wast thou taken: for dust thou *art*, and unto dust shalt thou return.

20 And Adam called his wife's name Eve; because she was the mother of all living.

21 Unto Adam also and to his wife did the Lord God make coats of skins, and clothed them.

22 And the Lord God said, Behold, the man is become as one of us, to know good and evil: and now, lest he put forth his hand, and take also of the tree of life, and eat, and live for ever:

23 Therefore the Lord God sent him forth from the garden of Eden, to till the ground from whence he was taken.

24 So he drove out the man; and he placed at the east of the garden of Eden Cherubims, and a flaming sword which turned every way, to keep the way of the tree of life.

CHAPTER IV.

AND Adam knew Eve his wife; and she conceived, and bare Cain, and said, I have gotten a man from the Lord.

2 And she again bare his brother Abel. And Abel was a keeper of sheep, but Cain was a tiller of the ground.

3 And in process of time it came to pass, that Cain brought of the fruit of the ground an offering unto the Lord.

4 And Abel, he also brought of the firstlings of his flock and of the fat thereof. And the Lord had respect unto Abel and to his offering:

5 But unto Cain and to his offering he had not respect. And Cain was very wroth, and his countenance fell.

6 And the Lord said unto Cain, Why art thou

וּבֵין זַרְעֲךָ הוּא יְשׁוּפְךָ רֹאשׁ וְאַתָּה תְּשׁוּפֶנּוּ
16 עָקֵב ׃ ס אֶל־הָאִשָּׁה אָמַר הַרְבָּה אַרְבֶּה עִצְּבוֹנֵךְ וְהֵרֹנֵךְ בְּעֶצֶב תֵּלְדִי בָנִים וְאֶל־אִישֵׁךְ תְּשׁוּקָתֵךְ וְהוּא יִמְשָׁל־בָּךְ ׃
17 וּלְאָדָם אָמַר כִּי שָׁמַעְתָּ לְקוֹל אִשְׁתֶּךָ וַתֹּאכַל מִן־הָעֵץ אֲשֶׁר צִוִּיתִיךָ לֵאמֹר לֹא תֹאכַל מִמֶּנּוּ אֲרוּרָה הָאֲדָמָה בַּעֲבוּרֶךָ
18 בְּעִצָּבוֹן תֹּאכֲלֶנָּה כֹּל יְמֵי חַיֶּיךָ ׃ וְקוֹץ וְדַרְדַּר
19 תַּצְמִיחַ לָךְ וְאָכַלְתָּ אֶת־עֵשֶׂב הַשָּׂדֶה ׃ בְּזֵעַת אַפֶּיךָ תֹּאכַל לֶחֶם עַד שׁוּבְךָ אֶל־הָאֲדָמָה כִּי מִמֶּנָּה לֻקָּחְתָּ כִּי־עָפָר אַתָּה וְאֶל־עָפָר
20 תָּשׁוּב ׃ וַיִּקְרָא הָאָדָם שֵׁם אִשְׁתּוֹ חַוָּה כִּי
21 הִוא הָיְתָה אֵם כָּל־חָי ׃ וַיַּעַשׂ יְהֹוָה אֱלֹהִים לְאָדָם וּלְאִשְׁתּוֹ כָּתְנוֹת עוֹר וַיַּלְבִּשֵׁם ׃ פ חמישי
22 וַיֹּאמֶר ׀ יְהֹוָה אֱלֹהִים הֵן הָאָדָם הָיָה כְּאַחַד מִמֶּנּוּ לָדַעַת טוֹב וָרָע וְעַתָּה ׀ פֶּן־יִשְׁלַח יָדוֹ וְלָקַח גַּם מֵעֵץ הַחַיִּים וְאָכַל וָחַי לְעֹלָם ׃
23 וַיְשַׁלְּחֵהוּ יְהֹוָה אֱלֹהִים מִגַּן־עֵדֶן לַעֲבֹד
24 אֶת־הָאֲדָמָה אֲשֶׁר לֻקַּח מִשָּׁם ׃ וַיְגָרֶשׁ אֶת־הָאָדָם וַיַּשְׁכֵּן מִקֶּדֶם לְגַן־עֵדֶן אֶת־הַכְּרֻבִים וְאֵת לַהַט הַחֶרֶב הַמִּתְהַפֶּכֶת לִשְׁמֹר אֶת־
IV דֶּרֶךְ עֵץ הַחַיִּים ׃ ס וְהָאָדָם יָדַע אֶת־חַוָּה אִשְׁתּוֹ וַתַּהַר וַתֵּלֶד אֶת־קַיִן
2 וַתֹּאמֶר קָנִיתִי אִישׁ אֶת־יְהֹוָה ׃ וַתֹּסֶף לָלֶדֶת אֶת־אָחִיו אֶת־הָבֶל וַיְהִי־הֶבֶל רֹעֵה צֹאן
3 וְקַיִן הָיָה עֹבֵד אֲדָמָה ׃ וַיְהִי מִקֵּץ יָמִים וַיָּבֵא קַיִן מִפְּרִי הָאֲדָמָה מִנְחָה לַיהֹוָה ׃
4 וְהֶבֶל הֵבִיא גַם־הוּא מִבְּכֹרוֹת צֹאנוֹ וּמֵחֶלְבֵהֶן
5 וַיִּשַׁע יְהֹוָה אֶל־הֶבֶל וְאֶל־מִנְחָתוֹ ׃ וְאֶל־קַיִן וְאֶל־מִנְחָתוֹ לֹא שָׁעָה וַיִּחַר לְקַיִן מְאֹד וַיִּפְּלוּ
6 פָנָיו ׃ וַיֹּאמֶר יְהֹוָה אֶל־קָיִן לָמָּה חָרָה לָךְ

wroth? and why is thy countenance fallen?

7 If thou doest well, shalt thou not be accepted? and if thou doest not well, sin lieth at the door. And unto thee *shall be* his desire, and thou shalt rule over him.

8 And Cain talked with Abel his brother: and it came to pass, when they were in the field, that Cain rose up against Abel his brother, and slew him.

9 And the LORD said unto Cain, Where *is* Abel thy brother? And he said, I know not: *Am* I my brother's keeper?

10 And he said, What hast thou done? the voice of thy brother's blood crieth unto me from the ground.

11 And now *art* thou cursed from the earth, which hath opened her mouth to receive thy brother's blood from thy hand;

12 When thou tillest the ground, it shall not henceforth yield unto thee her strength; a fugitive and a vagabond shalt thou be in the earth.

13 And Cain said unto the LORD, My punishment *is* greater than I can bear.

14 Behold, thou hast driven me out this day from the face of the earth; and from thy face shall I be hid; and I shall be a fugitive and a vagabond in the earth; and it shall come to pass, *that* everyone that findeth me shall slay me.

15 And the LORD said unto him, Therefore whosoever slayeth Cain, vengeance shall be taken on him sevenfold. And the LORD set a mark upon Cain, lest any finding him should kill him.

16 And Cain went out from the presence of the LORD, and dwelt in the land of Nod, on the east of Eden.

17 And Cain knew his wife; and she conceived, and bare Enoch: and he builded a city, and called the name of the city, after the name of his son, Enoch.

18 And unto Enoch was born Irad: and Irad begat Mehujael: and Mehujael begat Methusael: and Methusael begat Lamech.

19 And Lamech took unto him two wives: the name of the one *was* Adah, and the name of the other Zillah.

20 And Adah bare Jabal: he was the father of such as dwell in tents, and *of such as have* cattle.

21 And his brother's name *was* Jubal: he was the father of all such as handle the harp and organ.

22 And Zillah, she also bare Tubal-cain, an instructer of every artificer in brass and iron: and the sister of Tubal-cain *was* Naamah.

23 And Lamech said unto his wives, Adah and Zillah, Hear my voice; ye wives of Lamech, hearken unto my speech: for I have slain a man

וְלָמָּה נָפְלוּ פָנֶיךָ : הֲלוֹא אִם־תֵּיטִיב שְׂאֵת
וְאִם לֹא תֵיטִיב לַפֶּתַח חַטָּאת רֹבֵץ וְאֵלֶיךָ
תְּשׁוּקָתוֹ וְאַתָּה תִּמְשָׁל־בּוֹ : 5 וַיֹּאמֶר קַיִן אֶל־
הֶבֶל אָחִיו וַיְהִי בִּהְיוֹתָם בַּשָּׂדֶה וַיָּקָם קַיִן
אֶל־הֶבֶל אָחִיו וַיַּהַרְגֵהוּ : 6 וַיֹּאמֶר יְהֹוָה אֶל־
קַיִן אֵי הֶבֶל אָחִיךָ וַיֹּאמֶר לֹא יָדַעְתִּי הֲשֹׁמֵר
10 אָחִי אָנֹכִי : וַיֹּאמֶר מֶה עָשִׂיתָ קוֹל דְּמֵי אָחִיךָ
11 צֹעֲקִים אֵלַי מִן־הָאֲדָמָה : וְעַתָּה אָרוּר אָתָּה
מִן־הָאֲדָמָה אֲשֶׁר פָּצְתָה אֶת־פִּיהָ לָקַחַת
12 אֶת־דְּמֵי אָחִיךָ מִיָּדֶךָ : כִּי תַעֲבֹד אֶת־
הָאֲדָמָה לֹא־תֹסֵף תֵּת־כֹּחָהּ לָךְ נָע וָנָד
13 תִּהְיֶה בָאָרֶץ : וַיֹּאמֶר קַיִן אֶל־יְהֹוָה גָּדוֹל
14 עֲוֹנִי מִנְּשֹׂא : הֵן גֵּרַשְׁתָּ אֹתִי הַיּוֹם מֵעַל פְּנֵי
הָאֲדָמָה וּמִפָּנֶיךָ אֶסָּתֵר וְהָיִיתִי נָע וָנָד
15 בָאָרֶץ וְהָיָה כָל־מֹצְאִי יַהַרְגֵנִי : וַיֹּאמֶר לוֹ
יְהֹוָה לָכֵן כָּל־הֹרֵג קַיִן שִׁבְעָתַיִם יֻקָּם וַיָּשֶׂם
יְהֹוָה לְקַיִן אוֹת לְבִלְתִּי הַכּוֹת־אֹתוֹ כָּל־
16 מֹצְאוֹ : וַיֵּצֵא קַיִן מִלִּפְנֵי יְהֹוָה וַיֵּשֶׁב
17 בְּאֶרֶץ־נוֹד קִדְמַת־עֵדֶן : וַיֵּדַע קַיִן אֶת־
אִשְׁתּוֹ וַתַּהַר וַתֵּלֶד אֶת־חֲנוֹךְ וַיְהִי בֹּנֶה
עִיר וַיִּקְרָא שֵׁם הָעִיר כְּשֵׁם בְּנוֹ חֲנוֹךְ :
18 וַיִּוָּלֵד לַחֲנוֹךְ אֶת־עִירָד וְעִירָד יָלַד אֶת־
מְחוּיָאֵל וּמְחִיָּיאֵל יָלַד אֶת־מְתוּשָׁאֵל
19 וּמְתוּשָׁאֵל יָלַד אֶת־לָמֶךְ : וַיִּקַּח־לוֹ לֶמֶךְ
שְׁתֵּי נָשִׁים שֵׁם הָאַחַת עָדָה וְשֵׁם הַשֵּׁנִית
20 צִלָּה : וַתֵּלֶד עָדָה אֶת־יָבָל הוּא הָיָה אֲבִי
21 יֹשֵׁב אֹהֶל וּמִקְנֶה : וְשֵׁם אָחִיו יוּבָל הוּא הָיָה
22 אֲבִי כָּל־תֹּפֵשׂ כִּנּוֹר וְעוּגָב : וְצִלָּה גַם־הִוא
יָלְדָה אֶת־תּוּבַל קַיִן לֹטֵשׁ כָּל־חֹרֵשׁ נְחֹשֶׁת
23 וּבַרְזֶל וַאֲחוֹת תּוּבַל־קַיִן נַעֲמָה : וַיֹּאמֶר לֶמֶךְ
לְנָשָׁיו עָדָה וְצִלָּה שְׁמַעַן קוֹלִי נְשֵׁי לֶמֶךְ
הַאְזֵנָּה אִמְרָתִי כִּי אִישׁ הָרַגְתִּי לְפִצְעִי וְיֶלֶד

to my wounding, and a young man to my hurt.

24 If Cain shall be avenged sevenfold, truly Lamech seventy and sevenfold.

25 And Adam knew his wife again; and she bare a son, and called his name Seth: For God, *said she*, hath appointed me another seed instead of Abel, whom Cain slew.

26 And to Seth, to him also there was born a son; and he called his name Enos: then began men to call upon the name of the LORD.

CHAPTER V.

THIS *is* the book of the generations of Adam. In the day that God created man, in the likeness of God made he him;

2 Male and female created he them; and blessed them, and called their name Adam, in the day when they were created.

3 And Adam lived an hundred and thirty years, and begat *a son* in his own likeness, after his image; and called his name Seth:

4 And the days of Adam after he had begotten Seth were eight hundred years: and he begat sons and daughters:

5 And all the days that Adam lived were nine hundred and thirty years: and he died.

6 And Seth lived an hundred and five years, and begat Enos:

7 And Seth lived after he begat Enos eight hundred and seven years, and begat sons and daughters:

8 And all the days of Seth were nine hundred and twelve years: and he died.

9 And Enos lived ninety years, and begat Cainan:

10 And Enos lived after he begat Cainan eight hundred and fifteen years, and begat sons and daughters:

11 And all the days of Enos were nine hundred and five years: and he died.

12 And Cainan lived seventy years, and begat Mahalaleel:

13 And Cainan lived after he begat Mahalaleel eight hundred and forty years, and begat sons and daughters:

14 And all the days of Cainan were nine hundred and ten years: and he died.

15 And Mahalaleel lived sixty and five years, and begat Jared:

לְחַבֻּרָתִי ׃ כִּי שִׁבְעָתַיִם יֻקַּם־קָיִן וְלֶמֶךְ 24

שִׁבְעִים וְשִׁבְעָה ׃ וַיֵּדַע אָדָם עוֹד אֶת־אִשְׁתּוֹ 25

וַתֵּלֶד בֵּן וַתִּקְרָא אֶת־שְׁמוֹ שֵׁת כִּי שָׁת־לִי

אֱלֹהִים זֶרַע אַחֵר תַּחַת הֶבֶל כִּי הֲרָגוֹ קָיִן ׃

וּלְשֵׁת גַּם־הוּא יֻלַּד־בֵּן וַיִּקְרָא אֶת־שְׁמוֹ 26

אֱנוֹשׁ אָז הוּחַל לִקְרֹא בְּשֵׁם יְהֹוָה ׃ ס ששי

זֶה סֵפֶר תּוֹלְדֹת אָדָם בְּיוֹם בְּרֹא אֱלֹהִים v

אָדָם בִּדְמוּת אֱלֹהִים עָשָׂה אֹתוֹ ׃ זָכָר וּנְקֵבָה 2

בְּרָאָם וַיְבָרֶךְ אֹתָם וַיִּקְרָא אֶת־שְׁמָם אָדָם

בְּיוֹם הִבָּרְאָם ׃ וַיְחִי אָדָם שְׁלֹשִׁים וּמְאַת 3

שָׁנָה וַיּוֹלֶד בִּדְמוּתוֹ כְּצַלְמוֹ וַיִּקְרָא אֶת־שְׁמוֹ

שֵׁת ׃ וַיִּהְיוּ יְמֵי־אָדָם אַחֲרֵי הוֹלִידוֹ אֶת־שֵׁת 4

שְׁמֹנֶה מֵאֹת שָׁנָה וַיּוֹלֶד בָּנִים וּבָנוֹת ׃ וַיִּהְיוּ 5

כָּל־יְמֵי אָדָם אֲשֶׁר־חַי תְּשַׁע מֵאוֹת שָׁנָה

וּשְׁלֹשִׁים שָׁנָה וַיָּמֹת ׃ ס וַיְחִי־ 6

שֵׁת חָמֵשׁ שָׁנִים וּמְאַת שָׁנָה וַיּוֹלֶד אֶת־

אֱנוֹשׁ ׃ וַיְחִי־שֵׁת אַחֲרֵי הוֹלִידוֹ אֶת־אֱנוֹשׁ 7

שֶׁבַע שָׁנִים וּשְׁמֹנֶה מֵאוֹת שָׁנָה וַיּוֹלֶד בָּנִים

וּבָנוֹת ׃ וַיִּהְיוּ כָּל־יְמֵי־שֵׁת שְׁתֵּים עֶשְׂרֵה 8

שָׁנָה וּתְשַׁע מֵאוֹת שָׁנָה וַיָּמֹת ׃ ס

וַיְחִי אֱנוֹשׁ תִּשְׁעִים שָׁנָה וַיּוֹלֶד אֶת־קֵינָן ׃ 9

וַיְחִי אֱנוֹשׁ אַחֲרֵי הוֹלִידוֹ אֶת־קֵינָן חֲמֵשׁ 10

עֶשְׂרֵה שָׁנָה וּשְׁמֹנֶה מֵאוֹת שָׁנָה וַיּוֹלֶד בָּנִים

וּבָנוֹת ׃ וַיִּהְיוּ כָּל־יְמֵי אֱנוֹשׁ חָמֵשׁ שָׁנִים 11

וּתְשַׁע מֵאוֹת שָׁנָה וַיָּמֹת ׃ ס וַיְחִי 12

קֵינָן שִׁבְעִים שָׁנָה וַיּוֹלֶד אֶת־מַהֲלַלְאֵל ׃ וַיְחִי 13

קֵינָן אַחֲרֵי הוֹלִידוֹ אֶת־מַהֲלַלְאֵל אַרְבָּעִים

שָׁנָה וּשְׁמֹנֶה מֵאוֹת שָׁנָה וַיּוֹלֶד בָּנִים וּבָנוֹת ׃

וַיִּהְיוּ כָּל־יְמֵי קֵינָן עֶשֶׂר שָׁנִים וּתְשַׁע מֵאוֹת 14

שָׁנָה וַיָּמֹת ׃ ס וַיְחִי מַהֲלַלְאֵל 15

חָמֵשׁ שָׁנִים וְשִׁשִּׁים שָׁנָה וַיּוֹלֶד אֶת־יָרֶד ׃

וַיְחִי מַהֲלַלְאֵל אַחֲרֵי הוֹלִידוֹ אֶת־יָרֶד 16

16 And Mahalaleel lived after he begat Jared eight hundred and thirty years, and begat sons and daughters :

17 And all the days of Mahalaleel were eight hundred ninety and five years : and he died.

18 And Jared lived an hundred sixty and two years, and he begat Enoch :

19 And Jared lived after he begat Enoch eight hundred years, and begat sons and daughters :

20 And all the days of Jared were nine hundred sixty and two years : and he died.

21 And Enoch lived sixty and five years, and begat Methuselah :

22 And Enoch walked with God after he begat Methuselah three hundred years, and begat sons and daughters :

23 And all the days of Enoch were three hundred sixty and five years :

24 And Enoch walked with God : and he *was* not ; for God took him.

25 And Methuselah lived an hundred eighty and seven years, and begat Lamech :

26 And Methuselah lived after he begat Lamech seven hundred eighty and two years, and begat sons and daughters :

27 And all the days of Methuselah were nine hundred sixty and nine years : and he died.

28 And Lamech lived an hundred eighty and two years, and begat a son :

29 And he called his name Noah, saying, This *same* shall comfort us concerning our work and toil of our hands, because of the ground which the Lord hath cursed.

30 And Lamech lived after he begat Noah five hundred ninety and five years, and begat sons and daughters :

31 And all the days of Lamech were seven hundred seventy and seven years : and he died.

32 And Noah was five hundred years old : and Noah begat Shem, Ham, and Japheth.

CHAPTER VI.

AND it came to pass, when men began to multiply on the face of the earth, and daughters were born unto them,

2 That the sons of God saw the daughters of

שְׁלֹשִׁים שָׁנָה וּשְׁמֹנֶה מֵאוֹת שָׁנָה וַיּוֹלֶד
בָּנִים וּבָנוֹת: וַיִּהְיוּ כָּל־יְמֵי מַהֲלַלְאֵל חָמֵשׁ
וְתִשְׁעִים שָׁנָה וּשְׁמֹנֶה מֵאוֹת שָׁנָה וַיָּמֹת:
ס   וַיְחִי־יֶרֶד שְׁתַּיִם וְשִׁשִּׁים שָׁנָה
וּמְאַת שָׁנָה וַיּוֹלֶד אֶת־חֲנוֹךְ: וַיְחִי־יֶרֶד
אַחֲרֵי הוֹלִידוֹ אֶת־חֲנוֹךְ שְׁמֹנֶה מֵאוֹת
שָׁנָה וַיּוֹלֶד בָּנִים וּבָנוֹת: וַיִּהְיוּ כָּל־יְמֵי־
יֶרֶד שְׁתַּיִם וְשִׁשִּׁים שָׁנָה וּתְשַׁע מֵאוֹת שָׁנָה
וַיָּמֹת: ס   וַיְחִי חֲנוֹךְ חָמֵשׁ וְשִׁשִּׁים
שָׁנָה וַיּוֹלֶד אֶת־מְתוּשָׁלַח: וַיִּתְהַלֵּךְ חֲנוֹךְ
אֶת־הָאֱלֹהִים אַחֲרֵי הוֹלִידוֹ אֶת־מְתוּשֶׁלַח
שְׁלֹשׁ מֵאוֹת שָׁנָה וַיּוֹלֶד בָּנִים וּבָנוֹת: וַיְהִי
כָּל־יְמֵי חֲנוֹךְ חָמֵשׁ וְשִׁשִּׁים שָׁנָה וּשְׁלֹשׁ
מֵאוֹת שָׁנָה: וַיִּתְהַלֵּךְ חֲנוֹךְ אֶת־הָאֱלֹהִים
וְאֵינֶנּוּ כִּי־לָקַח אֹתוֹ אֱלֹהִים: ס   שביעי
וַיְחִי מְתוּשֶׁלַח שֶׁבַע וּשְׁמֹנִים שָׁנָה וּמְאַת
שָׁנָה וַיּוֹלֶד אֶת־לָמֶךְ: וַיְחִי מְתוּשֶׁלַח אַחֲרֵי
הוֹלִידוֹ אֶת־לֶמֶךְ שְׁתַּיִם וּשְׁמוֹנִים שָׁנָה
וּשְׁבַע מֵאוֹת שָׁנָה וַיּוֹלֶד בָּנִים וּבָנוֹת: וַיִּהְיוּ
כָּל־יְמֵי מְתוּשֶׁלַח תֵּשַׁע וְשִׁשִּׁים שָׁנָה וּתְשַׁע
מֵאוֹת שָׁנָה וַיָּמֹת: ס   וַיְחִי־לֶמֶךְ
שְׁתַּיִם וּשְׁמֹנִים שָׁנָה וּמְאַת שָׁנָה וַיּוֹלֶד בֵּן:
וַיִּקְרָא אֶת־שְׁמוֹ נֹחַ לֵאמֹר זֶה יְנַחֲמֵנוּ
מִמַּעֲשֵׂנוּ וּמֵעִצְּבוֹן יָדֵינוּ מִן־הָאֲדָמָה אֲשֶׁר
אֵרְרָהּ יְהוָה: וַיְחִי־לֶמֶךְ אַחֲרֵי הוֹלִידוֹ אֶת־
נֹחַ חָמֵשׁ וְתִשְׁעִים שָׁנָה וַחֲמֵשׁ מֵאֹת שָׁנָה
וַיּוֹלֶד בָּנִים וּבָנוֹת: וַיְהִי כָּל־יְמֵי־לֶמֶךְ
שֶׁבַע וְשִׁבְעִים שָׁנָה וּשְׁבַע מֵאוֹת שָׁנָה
וַיָּמֹת: ס   וַיְהִי־נֹחַ בֶּן־חֲמֵשׁ מֵאוֹת
שָׁנָה וַיּוֹלֶד נֹחַ אֶת־שֵׁם אֶת־חָם וְאֶת־יָפֶת:
וַיְהִי כִּי־הֵחֵל הָאָדָם לָרֹב עַל־פְּנֵי הָאֲדָמָה
וּבָנוֹת יֻלְּדוּ לָהֶם: וַיִּרְאוּ בְנֵי־הָאֱלֹהִים אֶת־

SUGGESTED READINGS
(Appendix B)

SUGGESTED BOOKS, DVD'S AND VIDEOS

1. *A Book of Hebrew Letters*, by Mark Podwal. Jewish Publication Society of America, Philadelphia, 1978.

2. *Adam and the Kabbalistic Tree*, by Shimon Halevi. Samuel Weiser, 1974.

3. *An Introduction to the Cabala*, by Shimon Halevi. Samuel Weiser, 1972.

4. *Fragments of a Future Scroll*, by Zalman Schachter. Leaves of Grass Press, Inc., 1975.

5. *Heritage: Civilization and the Jews* - Hosted by former Israeli Ambassador to the United States, Abba Eban. May buy as a Video or DVD Series. Features - Nine, one hour programs in a Deluxe five-tape boxed set. **http://www.jewishsoftware.com/products/328.asp**

6. *Israel: An Echo of Eternity*, by Abraham J. Heschel. Farrar, Straus, and Giroux, 1973.

7. *Kabbalah*, by Charles Poncé. Straight Arrow Books, 1973.

8. *Kabbalah*, by Gershom Scholem. Quadrangle/New York Times Book Company, 1974.

9. *Le Centre du Silence Work Book*, by Samuel Avital, self published, 1975.

10. *Le Centre du Silence Mime Work Book*, by Samuel Avital. Lotus Light Publications, 1982.

11. *Major Trends in Jewish Mysticism*, by Gershom Scholem. Schocken, 1969.

12. *Mime and Beyond: The Silent Outcry*, by Samuel Avital. Hohm Press, 1985.

13. *Mimenspiel* (The Mime Workbook, German Ed.), by Samuel Avital, 1985.

14. *On the Kabbalah and its Symbolism*, by Gershom Scholem. Schocken, 1970.

15. *OUT OF SPAIN: A Journey to Spain with Yitzhak Navon*

Eight (8) part documentary by the Israeli Broadcasting Television Documentaries.

A journey to Spain with Yitzhak Navon, the fifth President of the State of Israel. Episodes in the Series: The Spanish Connection, The Balance of Terror, The Inquisition, The Marranos, 1492, The Secret Jews of Portugal, The Eternal Jew of Majorca.

A 460-minute, Eight (8) episode videos in English. Item #8989-1 NTSC (USA) system. Price: $69.95 - Order From: Tal-Shahar, P.O. Box 1067, Tel Aviv 61009 ISRAEL. 4 Hayesod.
Email: **sales@tal-shahar.com** - Web site: **www.israel-catalog.com**

16. *Practical Kabbalah,* by Rabbi Laible Wolf. Three Rivers Press: New York, NY, 1999.

17. *Sepher Hazohar* with Hasullam translation and interpretation from Aramaic to Hebrew by Rabbi Yehua Lev Ashlag. (21 Volumes with vowels) Bnei Baruch, P.O. Box 584 Bnei Brak 51104 - Israel, 1998.
Phone: 972-55-606707, Fax: 972-3-9226924 $288.00
International website: **http://www.kabbalahbooks.info**
Hebrew website: **http://www.kabbalah,info/hebkab/index_heb.htm**

18. *The BodySpeak™ Manual,* by Samuel Avital. 1st Books, 2001.

19. *The Cipher of Genesis,* by Carlo Suares. Bantam Books, 1967.

20. *The Conception Mandala,* by Samuel Avital & Mark Olsen. Destiny Books, 1992.

21. *The Essential Kabbalah - The Heart of Jewish Mysticism,* by Daniel C. Matt. Castlenooks: Edison, NJ, 1995.

22. *The Hebrew Alphabet - A Mystical Journey,* by Edward Hoffman. Illustrations by Karen Silver. Chronicle Books: San Francisco, CA, 1988.

23. *The Path of the Just,* by Moshe Chayim Luzzatto. Translated by Shraga Silverstein. Feldheim Publishers: Jerusalem, Israel, 1966 & 1990.

SUGGESTED BOOKS, DVD'S AND VIDEOS CONT'D.

24. *The Silent Outcry - The Life & Times of Samuel Avital,* (Video), by Samuel Avital, 1992. (Available through Mr. Avital)

25. *The Wisdom in the Hebrew Alphabet,* by Rabbi Michael L. Munk. Mesorah Publications, Inc.: Brooklyn, NY, 2nd Ed., 1983.

26. *The Sabbath,* by Abraham J. Heschel. Noonday Press, 1975.

27. *The Sepher Yetsira,* by Carlo Suares. Shambhala, 1976.

28. *The Song of Songs,* by Carlo Suares. Shambhala, 1972.

29. *The Universal Meaning of the Kabbalah,* by Leo Schaya. Penguin, 1973.

30. *The Way of God,* by Moshe Chaim Luzzatto. Translated by Aryeh Kaplan. Feldheim Publishers: Jerusalem, Israel, 1997.

31. *The Wisdom of the Zohar (3 Volumes).* By Isaiah Tishby, Fischel Lachower and Translated from Hebrew by David Goldstein. The Littman Library of Jewish Civilization, London, 1994.

32. *The Zohar in Moslem and Christian Spain.* By Ariel Bension, Ph.D. Hermon Press: New York, NY, 1974.

33. *Zohar, The Book of Splendor, Basic Readings from the Kabbalah.* Edited by Gershom Scholem. Schocken, 1966.

HERITAGE OF FAMILIES
(Appendix C)

Heritage of my Families Abitbol, Ezekri, and Elbaz

My name is (Samuel) Shemuel Ben-Or Avital* of the house of Abitbol. I was born on the 23rd, in the month of Tevet, 1932, in Sefrou, (near Fez) Morocco, which was known then as "Little Jerusalem." As a son of the families Abitbol, Ezekri, and Elbaz, I write these words as a testament to my ancestors and for the lineage of the wise rabbis, kabbalists, and their spiritual heirs.

My family has three sacred branches of honor from the tree of wisdom, adding to the splendid heritage of our people. These are the families Abitbol, Ezekri, and Elbaz, may their light illumine us. These saints were revered by the honest and pure people of the "City of the Torah," Sefrou, but, were also known throughout Morocco and in many other parts of the world.

From the family Abitbol, branched many rabbis, judges, interpreters, spiritual leaders, and renown Mekoubalim, who were honored by the community, and, whose good name always walked before them in the world.

The Abitbol's were descendants of the Megorashim - exiled in 1492 of Castille. In the line, my father, Moshe Amram, and my beloved grandfather, Eliyahu Ya'akov, blessed be his memory, is the HaRav HaGa'on, Rabbi

Heritage of my Families Abitbol, Ezekri, and Elbaz Cont'd.

Amor Abitbol. He was an interpreter of the Torah, a Dayan, and giant of holiness in whom dwelt a true splendor of being. Author of "Omer Man" and "Shirat HaOmer" that was just re-published in Israel in a new edition.

Through my mother, Hannah Robidah and the family of Ezekri, there were also many learned and wise kabbalists of great vision, such as the author of the "Sefer Haredim," Rabbi Eliezer Ezekri, blessed be his memory. He was a disciple of the Great ARI, Rabbi Hayim Vital, and Cordovero in Tsafet, the city of kabbalists, at the time.

The family of Elbaz is well-known, and according to a tradition that comes from Syria, the family of Abu-Hatsirah is in truth Elbaz (Abu-Hatsirah being a name given to Rabbi Shemuel Elbaz Z"L after the miraculous event he was known to have caused). Rabbi Shemuel Elbaz was famous as a powerful healer throughout the world. Many people still visit his place of burial to ask for healing.

Now, my mother, Hannah Robidah, was the daughter of Simha, who was the daughter of the great Rabbi, Abba Elbaz, blessed be his memory. He was a great rabbi and teacher of justice, for many years a judge and posek, one who decides on how to interpret the halachah. He said once, that my mother Hannah Robidah, the beloved and merciful of the family Ezekri, will be blessed with good family and children.

Heritage of my Families Abitbol, Ezekri, and Elbaz Cont'd.

The cousin of Rabbi Abba Elbaz was the great Rabbi Raphael Moshe Elbaz, called RAMA (his acronym). He was a great visionary, miracle maker, and famed kabbalist, who authored many classic books like, "The Ancient from Eden," "Things of Sweetness," "The Four Guardians," "The Crown of Gold," "The Words of Moshe," "New Songs," "Throne of Kings," "The Seven Wisdoms," and many other works that are still in manuscript form. Some well published today.

He was a poet of great renown, and a kabbalist of great powers, a revered miracle maker whose beautiful songs in the style of the classic Andalusian music are marked by a marvelous depth and content, and have become prayers, used many Jewish Sephardim communities around the world, and some of which included in the repertoire of the Israeli Andalusian Orchestra.

* I changed my name to AVITAL when I was in the Kibbutz, Ayelet Hashahar (high Galilee) in 1949, the year I immigrated to Israel - (March 20, 1949). I now use the name of Samuel Avital.

Samuel Avital, Founder and Director
Le Centre du Silence Mime School

Website: http://www.bodyspeak.com

BIOGRAPHY OF
SAMUEL BEN-OR AVITAL
(Appendix D)

Biography of Samuel Ben-Or Avital
"He teaches a Kabbalistic Tai-Chi in which God and Man are fused in MIME."
Reb Zalman Schachter-Shalomi

Samuel Ben-Or Avital was born in a small village **Sefrou,** near **Fez,** in the Atlas Mountains of Morocco. He was educated in the home of a simple and remarkable family, which traces its lineage to **15th Century Spain** and before. Carrying from father to son is an unbroken line, in the **Sephardic tradition,** the ancient, beautiful and practical wisdom of the Hebrew Science of the **Kabbalah.**

At a young age, Samuel embarked on the first of many adventurous journeys, which led him to Israel and later to Paris, France, Europe and Scandinavia to the United States. During his travels from East to West, Samuel encountered and explored different schools of knowledge, including Alchemical and Sufi traditions, which he absorbed, and later synthesized into his own organic and Cosmic Kabbalistic learning.

Biography of Samuel Ben-Or Avital Cont'd.

Over the years, he accumulated the knowledge of a few languages, which assisted him to live in the Western world. At the age of 14, Samuel traveled to Israel where he spent ten years, living in a kibbutz, and other schools, which included the study of physics, agronomy, theology, arts and theatre. He performed in many countries and shared his knowledge to all who orbited in his vicinity. He toured in North and South America, Canada, and in 1969, he was invited to teach Mime and Movement Theatre as an Artist-in-Residence at SMU, Dallas, Texas.

His innate interest in the arts eventually drew him to Paris where he studied with mime master, Etienne Decroux. Having met his art form, Avital threw himself into what he found to be the very essence of human expression. Decroux, Barrault, and Marceau were all to have a profound influence on the formation of his own artistic expression. He soon began touring with Maximilien Decroux and was also, doing solo performances.

In 1964, Samuel joined his friend Moni Yakim in New York, performing with him in his Pantomime Theatre of New York and, also, in the off off-Broadway theatres, as well as, teaching mime in New York City schools. Later, he toured in North and South America and Canada. In 1969, he was invited to teach at SMU in Dallas.

Biography of Samuel Ben-Or Avital Cont'd.

In 1971, he established **Le Centre du Silence Mime School** in Boulder, Colorado. The following year, he created the **Boulder Mime Theatre (BMT)** with his most dedicated students. The **BMT** performed during the next 12 years in local, state and national engagements.

In 1975, Avital initiated the **International Summer Mime Workspace,** an annual intensive course attracting students worldwide. The same year, he published his *MIME WORKBOOK* followed by a second edition in 1977, a third printing in 1982, and *MIMENSPIEL,* a German edition published in Frankfurt, Germany. Hohm Press of Prescott, Arizona, published his second book, *MIME & BEYOND: The Silent Outcry* in 1985. Inner Traditions, Rochester, VT, published *The CONCEPTION MANDALA* by Samuel Avital and Mark Olsen. His video, *The Silent Outcry: The Life and Times of Samuel Avital* was produced in 1992, and, is available via Le Centre du Silence. In 1985, he was nominated for the Colorado Governor's Award for Excellence in the Arts.

His book, *The BodySpeak Manual*™, published in August, 2001, is NOW available as an electronic book and print on demand. The new edition, published in 2015, can be ordered via Amazon.com.

Samuel's book, *"THE INVISIBLE STAIRWAY • Kabbalistic Meditations on the Hebrew Letters,"* was first published by **Aleph-Beith Publishers** in 1982 in Boulder, Colorado. The second, private publication by **Kol-Emeth Publishers** was revised and completed in Hebrew and English versions in 2003. This new edition of the English version, published by **Le Centre du Silence** in 2016, is the first public edition, and is available via Amazon.com.

Over the years, Samuel developed his unique method of teaching, and created *BodySpeak™* training. He has also contributed numerous articles, interviews and essays in several languages to diverse publications throughout the U.S. and abroad.

Currently, Avital lives in Lafayette, Colorado where he continues his artistic activities and offers his **Kabbalistic gatherings, Tikkun Assemblies,** and *BodySpeak™* workshops in the U.S. and Europe.

For more information and program training, write, call, email or visit Le Centre du Silence website.

Le Centre du Silence, Samuel Avital, Director
P.O. Box 745, Lafayette, Colorado 80026 U.S.A.
savital@bodyspeak.com
www.bodyspeak.com
www.gokabbalahnow.com
©1971-2016 Samuel Avital, Le Centre du Silence, Lafayette, Colorado, USA.

.....AND CREATED THE UNIVERSE WITH THREE SEFARIM
(Appendix E)

"...וברא את עולמו בשלשה ספרים בספר וספר"

ספר יצירה פרק א - משנה א.

"...And created the universe with three sefarim" - Sepher Yetzirah 1.1.

"In the Beginning was the word, before the word there was movement.
Movement is vibration, life, vision, the stuff of creation,
and the essence of everything.
An intelligent being thinks and talks.
An emotional being sings.
A totally integrated and conscious BEING,
thinks, talks, sings, moves, and ACTS."

Samuel Avital in a public lecture/workshop, Boulder, Colorado, 1978

In the first verse of the Sepher Yetzirah, **ספר יצירה**
(The Book of Formation) it is written:

...וברא את עולמו בשלשה ספרים בספר וספורוספר.

ספר יצירה פרק א ' משנה א.

....."And created the universe with three Sefarim" - **ספרים** namely:

1. Sphar - **סְפָר** = number
2. Sippour - **סִפּוּר** = story, and
3. Sepher - **סֵפֶר** = book, which they are in reality <u>one, different,</u> and <u>the same.</u>

These similar word expressions of Sepharim **ספר** with the same root

of Samekh **ס** Pe **פ** and Reish **ר** have the following meaning:

1.) Number, calculation and/or idea;
2.) The story of the word or narrative;
3.) The writing of the word, the idea, the book.

"...And Created the Universe with Three Sefarim" Cont'd.

Human thinking have words that describe reality. The "**thing**" is not actually **the thing itself.** For example, the word "**water**" is not actual water. You can shout the word "**water**" in the desert, but you do not have the real water to drink to save your life.

To the Creator's "**way of thinking,**" the idea, the thought, the word, the action, and writing, are all ONE and the SAME. Meaning, when the Creator utters the word "WATER," there is the **actuality** and the **manifestation** of WATER, and your life is saved.

When the Kabbalist, who achieves total alignment with the Creator, he then, becomes the "**Complete Human.**" Now, when our "**Complete Human**" utters the word "WATER," when it is absolutely necessary, behold! there is water to drink, and **LIFE is saved.** We humans, call that natural manifestation "**a miracle.**"

And no wonder, that some Kabbalists ARE "Miracle Makers." And even then, ONLY when there is an absolute necessity, and not to demonstrate their "**powers,**" and they are "given permission" to **ACT** in alignment with the **"ONE WHO UTTERED THE WORD and THE WORLD IS."**

It is known also to Kabbalists that the thought, the speech and the action are one and the same in the Creator and with all creation. This is what I

"...And Created the Universe with Three Sefarim" Cont'd.

call, *"The journey from Thought to Action,"* מחשבה דיבור ומעשה הכל הוא דבר

אחד בבורא. Also, סוף מעשה במחשבה תחילה "The end of the action is in the

thought first." Before any action, there must be a thought.

This emphasis focuses on the idea, that the word and the work are **ONE**

and **the SAME** with the Creator. This sensible world was made and created

with these ideals, and there is definitely a difference between the way

humans think and do. We call **"The Creator"** the essence creative force of

BEING. This separates the way humans think from the way the "Creator"

thinks and creates. As it was expressed by the Prophets of Israel, "My

thoughts are not like yours."

So, one can aspire to evolve to another sphere of thinking and doing that

is **"beyond"** human, and is also very human and being **"like"** The Creator.

Let's first say according to this understanding that: In the beginning was

the dot, the Yod (י), the source of all ideas, writings, forms, and shapes.

Hence, to form a letter, a sign with intelligence so we can share the oneness

of all creation.

Yod (י) is the beginning of the beginning, the beginnings of the end, and

the end of all ends and the end of all beginnings. This in Kabbalah is called,

"...And Created the Universe with Three Sefarim" Cont'd.

Ein-Sof (אין-סוף), no-end, infinity, or **"That which cannot be talked about,"** defined with words and concepts, that which can ONLY be experienced with total understanding through the expressions, emanations and manifestations of the עשר ספירות, Ten (10), Yod (י) Sephiroth.

This is why, the root of the Hebrew letters are of great importance to **relate, unite, shape, form, create,** which can make worlds or destroy them. This depends upon the degree of intelligence, awakened awareness and consciousness that was invested within a person - **The process of being and becoming.**

So, from the dot to the line, to the letter, to the sentence, to the phrase, to the page, to the book, a "cover" is formed = a body. From a cell to an organ, the shape and form, to the whole organism, the body becomes animated or inanimated, conscious or unconscious, emerging into existence. We use letters to form the word, to write books, to tell our story while passing through time, space and matter, manifesting reality from the invisible.

Now we may say:

1. When you will learn and know the essential meaning of the Hebrew letters and learn to "read" and understand the true significance of

"...And Created the Universe with Three Sefarim" Cont'd.

Aleph, you will walk and you will learn to walk and move safely.

2. When you walk and know their "hidden" significance, they will "reveal" to you the "hidden" meaning of the universe, and the purpose of Creation, and how to influence events, thoughts and actions.

3. The form of the letters will not just be signs on the white sheet of paper, static and still. They will emerge alive and moving. You will sense the dynamic movements of each letter and how they relate and express the most complicated concept with simplicity and utter obviousness. With this practical knowledge, you will be able to build and create worlds with ease.

4. The Hebrew letters will also teach you how to relate to "this world," "understand" and "deal" with "seeming" chaos, complexities and the utter simplicity of creation.

EMET MANDALA
(Appendix F)

EMET MANDALA

EMET in Hebrew is meant to reflect, in the language of man, TRUTH. It is formed with three stone (letters) to build the concept of beginning, middle and end in regard to the measuring time of man on the physical plane.

ALEPH and MEM form the concept of Motherhood, source of all living. MEM and TAV form the concept of "death," the transition from room to room according to the Zohar. Thus, we can say that Birth, Life and Death are connected on all levels. It also depicts the concept of TAV and MEM, which means Purity, Simplicity and Completion. It has the stamp of perfection and what we call the "Sacred Innocence."

TAV and ALEPH means, from our roots, to be the "cell," the original cell of creation as the truth of being and becoming. All the web of the universe is connected by the design of the triangle, which is the symbol of perfection and simplicity. The computation of the holy name is woven into each of the six small triangles of the big one.

Wheels into wheels, lines and circles coming into the harmony of the truth in each cell that makes the whole. The letters, visible but invisible in the same breath, aid us to try to comprehend this concept, and live it in our own cellular organism in the "Sacred Innocence" and completion of the work we came to this world to accomplish.

The Center is the "Great Name," surrounded by all the letters in the embrace of the one in all and the all in one, and it expands in all directions to reach all who need to drink from the "Holy Fountain."

The circular movement of the design suggests that this oneness, is here, and all we need to do is to open our hearts to the OBVIOUSNESS of TRUTH in every level of our lives.

As Ben Bag Bag would say, **"Turn it and turn it, for all is in it, and look deeply within and grow old and grey in it, and turn not away from it, for there is no better rule for you than it."** *Pirke Avoth, Chapter 5, Verse 21.*

EMET MANDALA

THE SHIELD OF THE BELOVED
(Appendix G)

The Shield of the Beloved

In this introduction to what is called in Kabbalah, "The Divine Mirror," or, "The Diamond Within," I am addressing myself both to the one within who knows, and to the one within who is ignorant. I will try to speak a language that reaches everyone. There is nothing new here, it is very simple.

We begin with a symbol to put these ideas in focus. The symbol itself is a form of focusing the left side of the brain so we can cross over to the right side and create marriage of ourselves in understanding what it is we're all about, and what we are doing here on the way to forming the symbol called, "The Shield of the Beloved," a very simple symbol in the shape of an hour glass.

There is a lower pyramid and an upper inverted pyramid, and a place of connection between the two. In the Kabbalah, these two pyramids or triangles represent the "lower world" and the "upper world." The lower world is the finite world. The world of matter, the physical, the tangible, the world that is known, the world of Being. It is where we are when we are born from nowhere to something. The upper world is called the "Ein Sof," the world of the infinite, the unconscious, the world of the spirit, the unknown world, the world of Becoming.

Now, each of these worlds, the lower and the upper, have ten stairs or steps which are the stairs of ascending evolution. The bottom three stairs of the lower pyramid represents the mineral, the vegetable, the animal and human kingdoms, with their own different rungs and levels. Most of humanity, almost all, 99.9% of humanity, are here on these bottom three steps.

The Shield of the Beloved Cont'd.

The purpose of being here in this world is to ascend the ten steps of the lower pyramid of being, of learning to be, to the upper pyramid, the pyramid of becoming.

But, you cannot ascend these steps directly. You must take an "invisible stairway," a spiraling stairway that is multi-dimensional. Not like a ladder that you just walk up, but, where you have to turn around and around, and swirl and whirl in the air or in the understanding to get from one space of a rung to another.

This inner, invisible, multi-dimensional stairway is the channel - the funneling process as it is called in the Kabbalah. The funnel through which ideas, manifestations of the upper world come to the lower world to teach us, to show us this or that, inventions of scientists, and so on. Everything comes through this. It is the Passage, the birth canal. It is the "Ladder of Jacob," the ladder of earth and heaven. It forms the tubes of communication from the lower world to the upper, from the upper world to the lower.

But the area where the upper part of the hour-glass unites with the lower part of the hour-glass is a very dangerous sphere, a cross road, a flame. It is very trying and very difficult. It has been called, "the dark night of the soul."

It is the revolving door of the Garden of Eden, and if you are unaware for even one minute, it is goodbye for now and see you next incarnation. We sometimes visit this place, but, can't get through. It is so narrow, that if our ego is too fat with all its extra baggage, we won't get through. We have to get thin for that.

The Shield of the Beloved Cont'd.

Very few dare to try to get through. For all of this is unknown to us, and we are afraid. We whirl around in the world of the known, learning how to be, learning the physical primal things, learning how to eat and walk and make love and deal with this world, paying rent, dealing with stuff, with matter.

To get through that place where the upper meets the lower is to be cooked in the cauldron where the ego gets burned, though, not to ashes - the alchemical "tannoor," the furnace. You have to be cooked to pass through there, to absorb that heat and get used to it.

You need a Master's card, a VISA, to go through there, which means acquiring certain tools and mastering them. You have to master visualization through repeated practice. First of all, you have to be able to quickly push the button into the Inspiration World and create. And, you must have a realization of the "Infinite Being of Light" within you. If you don't have that, you can't pass through here.

You must have Total Sanity. You must walk Sane in the Midst of Madness, in a world gone off balance, almost to the point of no return. You can't wait for he or she to love you and kiss you and all of that. That's for lower humanity. We're talking about ways and means so we can climb and spiral up to that sphere where we came from, which is our Source. Where once upon a time, we were particles of light that got dropped from above to below.

Somehow, we got the application of where to incarnate and got picked up by a man and woman in union and....phht...it got born. It forgets once upon a time it was light. It is trapped in the physical organism, and forgets.

The Shield of the Beloved Cont'd.

And that's the purpose. The lower triangle is the school of remembering. It's the cosmic theatre where all the egos come about and all the attractions of the polarities happen. It is a world of doubt, and we need the Sanity of Certainty to pass beyond it. You can't pass through if you doubt.

That's a lot to ask of us primates on this planet, I know, but it's better to ask that, than a raise from your boss. Here you raise your self, not your salary. You must have total Awakening, total Awareness for your cosmic VISA. All these items you must get for your self. Down here, you write your own script, you author your self and do the lead acting - the activity of it, always with words in this world of words.

We talk and talk, but, some of us learn to acquire the cosmic VISA. Then, we know how to swirl and whirl, dealing with this and that. And if we say "I love you," we know what's going on. We know who this "I" is, and, who is this "you." We then know what love is, and, what this separation is between "you" and "I."

When we say, "I am hungry," we know "I am" is never hungry. The stomach is hungry. We can make distinctions. We learn how to transcend the male and female aspects and all the polarities. Otherwise, no entrance, and no exit. Otherwise, we're stuck here for millions of years incarnating, coming back and coming back down here where the cooking happens - in all the relationships, all the petty things we do, the fathers and daughters, mothers and sons, the states and nations. If we get caught in the cooking, we may not have the feast of passing through all this.

So, it is that some of us focused, units of consciousness, of light, depending on our inner velocity and voltage and degree of awareness and awakening, get SUCKED

The Shield of the Beloved Cont'd.

UP into the upper pyramid. Perhaps unconsciously or accidentally, we remember for an instant, and then maybe it happens again, we get SUCKED UP into that reservoir of knowledge of becoming until we learn we can do that consciously, with practice, until we ourselves become channels of communication, teachers, artists, inventors, helpers of mankind.

That means we got used to the heat of the cooking. All the right ingredients, the water boiling just right, the cosmic recipe in the works... And something starts to happen that begins to make sense. We crack the cosmic code. The ladder, the invisible stairway, gets shorter and shorter as we learn the routes. The triangles merge, infusing the upper with the lower. The lower becoming comfortable with the upper.

Here is the visibility of it, the center of being and becoming, the Jewel of the Kabbalah, the Shield of the Beloved. This is the yes and no, the dark and the light, the center of the heart. The state of total protection where you can walk on water if you want, or become a millionaire. You can overcome great difficulties in this sphere of certainty according to your benevolent intentions.

Until that can happens, you stay down here with the rest of humanity in the lower triangle, in the pyramid of limited time and space, with its arguments and divisions, philosophies and religions. Everyone pretending to know this or being that. Always pretending. Pretending to communicate. Talking when it is unnecessary with words that have no real value.

The Shield of the Beloved Cont'd.

There's no use pretending. That won't generate the voltage you need, the VISA. Human consciousness is a container of light, and you need the proper voltage and frequency to be sucked up there at will (though you do it every night while you sleep and when you die. Sleep is the time when you learn how to die, according to the Zohar) merging time and the timeless. That is the Jewel. That is ALEPH.

The Kabbalah says that Aleph exists in all the letters of the alphabet and all the letters exist in Aleph. Only in Aleph, is there the possibility to express Unity, the One without a second. That is why Aleph is constructed with a diagonal line.

That oblique line means in time and out of time together, as in the Divine Mirror. The invisibility of the upper reflected in the visibility of the lower. Aleph says we are already here and there. The upper and lower world are one in the same. As above, so below. We are already enlightened. Aleph says we have to learn that, because we have forgotten. And we can stand the heat of it, if we do not pretend.

But, to ascend in the remembering of that enlightenment, we first have to acknowledge the hiddenness of our "endarkenment." Endarkenment is when the light first descends into the body, the cellular organism. Inside the body all is dark. You can't realize the light until you know the darkness - all that you hide, all that you think nobody sees, the negative side, the shadow. You have to dare to face that. That is endarkenment, which is also enlightenment. They are one in the same.

You are a human being, you are a human becoming. The journey takes you to the edge of nothingness. Go carefully. Be well prepared. And the sadness you meet on the way, remember to enjoy it.

Samuel Avital, Boulder, CO - 1982

ADON HAKOL ILLUSTRATION

I Will BE what I will BE

אֶהְיֶה אֲשֶׁר אֶהְיֶה

I WILL BE WHAT I WILL BE

This EHYEH ASHER EHYEH illustration is an attempt to
understand the understandable. to try to grasp the ungraspable.
To understand the dot, the line, the form, the volume
and the essence of the raw material of Creation.

To understand the process of formation and the use
of the great infinite conscious intelligence,
To feel how to manifest what is "hidden"
within all created beings.
To learn how to see the "invisible" and BE in the "visible".

This illustration is a silent outcry of form and no form,
alleys, triangles, pathways, hidden gateways
toward that realization of BECOMING
close to the CREATOR and JUST BE...

Simply a human attempt to unveil little from the hidden
and LET THERE BE LIGHT in every heart and soul that
is aware and alert to the new possibilities,
so that every "dark" sphere of existence may swim in
the light of BEING AND BECOMING.

A modest offering for those who know to make
the conscious and directed efforts
to learn how to learn
to learn to see how to see
to learn to hear how to hear
to learn to feel how to feel
to learn to touch how to touch
to learn to be how to be
to learn to become how to become.

Thank you for BEING and BECOMING, HERE AND NOW.

Samuel Ben-Or Avital

אֶהְיֶה אֲשֶׁר אֶהְיֶה

I WILL BE WHAT I WILL BE

The Cosmic declaration of BEING
The Infinite Utterance of BEING and BECOMING
The identity of infinite intelligence and BEINGNESS.

The Cosmic Command of Existence
The Proclamation of infinite intelligence
The complete knowlege of BEING in all infinite dimensions.

Beingness in all forms, thoughts and actions
Constant movements in all invisible and visible worlds
The potent power buried deep in the GRAIN of BEING.

The inner movements that nurtures all living possibilities
The power of LOVE that permeates everyone
The power of LIFE that makes ONE BE and BECOME.

The following Hebrew words are inscribed
inside the circles in this illustration.

אֲדוֹן הַכֹּל

הוּא הָיָה הוּא הֹוֶה הוּא יִהְיֶה

אָנָּא הָאֵל יוֹצֵר הַכֹּל

יַחַד הוֹדְךָ וְזִיו הַדָּרְךָ עַל כֹּל

אֵל מִסְתַּתֵּר בְּשַׁפְרִיר חֶבְיוֹן

הַשֵּׂכֶל הַנֶּעֱלָם מִכֹּל רַעְיוֹן

עִילַת הָעִילוֹת מוּכְתָּר בְּכֶתֶר עֶלְיוֹן

Psalms 23*

1. A psalm of David. The Lord is my shepherd, I shall not want.
2. In pastures of tender grass he causeth me to lie down: beside still waters he leadeth me.
3. My soul he refresheth; he guideth me in the tracks of righteousness for the sake of his name.
4. Yea, though I walk through the valley of the shadow of death, I will not fear evil; for thou art with me: thy rod and thy staff - they indeed comfort me.
5. Thou preparest before me a table in the presence of my assailants; thou anointest with oil my head: my cup overfloweth.
6. Surely, only goodness and kindness shall follow me all the days of my life: and I shall dwell in the house of the Lord to the utmost length of days.

Psalms 67

1. To the chief musician on Neginoth, a psalm or song.
2. May God be gracious unto us, and bless us; may he cause his face to shine upon us. Selah.
3. That upon earth men may know thy way, among all nations thy salvation.
4. The people will thank thee, O God; the people, all of them together will thank thee.
5. Nations will rejoice and sing for joy: when thou judgest the people righteously, and guidest the nations upon earth. Selah.
6. The people will thank thee, O God; the people, all of them together, will thank thee.
7. The earth yieldeth her products: (yea,) God, our own God, will bless us.
8. God will bless us: and all the ends of the earth shall fear him.

Psalms 121

1. A song for the degrees. I lift up my eyes unto the mountains: whence shall come my help?
2. My help is from the Lord, the maker of heaven and earth.
3. He will not suffer thy foot to slip: thy keeper doth not slumber.
4. Behold, he slumbereth not, and he sleepeth not - the keeper of Israel.
5. The Lord is thy keeper: the Lord is thy shade, he is on thy right hand.
6. By day the sun shall not strike thee, nor the moon by night.
7. The Lord will guard thee against all evil; he will guard thy soul.
8. The Lord will guard thy going out and thy coming in from this time forth and for evermore.

*Note: These three psalms are the verses inside the three triangles of the Adon Hakol illustration.

שלשה פרקי תהלים

פרק כג

א. מִזְמוֹר לְדָוִד יְהֹוָה רֹעִי לֹא אֶחְסָר

ב. בִּנְאוֹת דֶּשֶׁא יַרְבִּיצֵנִי עַל־מֵי מְנֻחוֹת יְנַהֲלֵנִי׃

ג. נַפְשִׁי יְשׁוֹבֵב יַנְחֵנִי בְמַעְגְּלֵי־צֶדֶק לְמַעַן שְׁמוֹ׃

ד. גַּם כִּי־אֵלֵךְ בְּגֵיא צַלְמָוֶת לֹא־אִירָא רָע כִּי־אַתָּה עִמָּדִי שִׁבְטְךָ וּמִשְׁעַנְתֶּךָ הֵמָּה יְנַחֲמֻנִי׃

ה. תַּעֲרֹךְ לְפָנַי ׀ שֻׁלְחָן נֶגֶד צֹרְרָי דִּשַּׁנְתָּ בַשֶּׁמֶן רֹאשִׁי כּוֹסִי רְוָיָה׃

ו. אַךְ ׀ טוֹב וָחֶסֶד יִרְדְּפוּנִי כָּל־יְמֵי חַיָּי וְשַׁבְתִּי בְּבֵית־יְהֹוָה לְאֹרֶךְ יָמִים׃

פרק סז

א. לַמְנַצֵּחַ בִּנְגִינֹת מִזְמוֹר שִׁיר׃

ב. אֱלֹהִים יְחָנֵּנוּ וִיבָרְכֵנוּ יָאֵר פָּנָיו אִתָּנוּ סֶלָה׃

ג. לָדַעַת בָּאָרֶץ דַּרְכֶּךָ בְּכָל־גּוֹיִם יְשׁוּעָתֶךָ׃

ד. יוֹדוּךָ עַמִּים ׀ אֱלֹהִים יוֹדוּךָ עַמִּים כֻּלָּם׃

ה. יִשְׂמְחוּ וִירַנְּנוּ לְאֻמִּים כִּי־תִשְׁפֹּט עַמִּים מִישֹׁר וּלְאֻמִּים ׀ בָּאָרֶץ תַּנְחֵם סֶלָה׃

ו. יוֹדוּךָ עַמִּים ׀ אֱלֹהִים יוֹדוּךָ עַמִּים כֻּלָּם׃

ז. אֶרֶץ נָתְנָה יְבוּלָהּ יְבָרְכֵנוּ אֱלֹהִים אֱלֹהֵינוּ׃

ח. יְבָרְכֵנוּ אֱלֹהִים וְיִירְאוּ אֹתוֹ כָּל־אַפְסֵי־אָרֶץ׃

פרק קכא

א. שִׁיר לַמַּעֲלוֹת אֶשָּׂא עֵינַי אֶל־הֶהָרִים מֵאַיִן יָבֹא עֶזְרִי׃

ב. עֶזְרִי מֵעִם יְהֹוָה עֹשֵׂה שָׁמַיִם וָאָרֶץ׃

ג. אַל־יִתֵּן לַמּוֹט רַגְלֶךָ אַל־יָנוּם שֹׁמְרֶךָ׃

ד. הִנֵּה לֹא־יָנוּם וְלֹא יִישָׁן שׁוֹמֵר יִשְׂרָאֵל׃

ה. יְהֹוָה שֹׁמְרֶךָ יְהֹוָה צִלְּךָ עַל־יַד יְמִינֶךָ׃

ו. יוֹמָם הַשֶּׁמֶשׁ לֹא־יַכֶּכָּה וְיָרֵחַ בַּלָּיְלָה׃

ז. יְהֹוָה יִשְׁמָרְךָ מִכָּל־רָע יִשְׁמֹר אֶת־נַפְשֶׁךָ׃

ח. יְהֹוָה יִשְׁמָר־צֵאתְךָ וּבוֹאֶךָ מֵעַתָּה וְעַד־עוֹלָם׃

Made in United States
Troutdale, OR
01/18/2025

28098390R00213